ANGELS OF CHAOS

A Journey Into the Dark Depths of the Human Psyche

MIGUEL F. BROOKS

FOR MATURE READERS ONLY

LMH PUBLISHING LIMITED

Editor: Tyrone S. Reid
Cover design: Sanya Dockery
Book design, layout & typesetting: Sanya Dockery

Published by LMH Publishing Limited
Suite 10-11, Sagicor Industrial Complex
7 Norman Road, Kingston C.S.O., Jamaica
Tel.: (876) 938-0005; 938-0712 • Fax: (876) 759-8752
Email: lmhbookpublishing@cwjamaica.com • Website: www.lmhpublishing.com

Printed in the U. S. A.

National Library of Jamaica Cataloguing-in-Publication Data

Brooks, Miguel F.
    Angels of Chaos: A Journey Into the Dark Depths of the Human Psyche
    p. ; cm
ISBN: 978-976-8202-64-2
1. Mental Illness   2.   Psychology, Pathological
I. Title
616.89   dc 22

To you, my clients, for you came to me for help, and in helping you, I learnt the true meaning of compassion, forgiveness, empathy and love. May the storms of your mind vanish as you enter that inner peace that lives within…that peace which never vanishes…

CONTENTS

FOREWORD

ANGELS OF CHAOS: A Journey Into the Dark Depths of the Human Psyche is an explicit and disturbing look at the dark side of the human psyche, presented through a collection of utterly fascinating abnormal psychology cases.

Clinical and research psychologist Miguel Brooks takes us deep into the minds of sexual sadists and predators, psychopaths, obsessive-compulsive and mood-disordered persons, as well as the guilt-burdened, depressed suicidal, and the twisted weirdoes we all encounter but often fail to understand.

Taken from his extensive clinical diaries, these chronicles reveal, in unusual and impacting detail, the harrowing psycho-emotional descent into a desperate hell, known only to those who have been there.

A condensed version of his Inner Mind trilogy, Angels of Chaos is written in a blunt but compassionate stance, in which Brooks attempts to gently coax our sensitivity and empathy, particularly those of us caught in the mind-bending vortex of cruel and unforgiving psychopathologies.

ACKNOWLEDGEMENT

I want to express my sincere thanks to everyone who contributed to the successful completion of this work by providing helpful suggestions, opinions and timely reviews of the early manuscript drafts. I must also extend a very special word of gratitude to those who read through what is admittedly an emotionally jarring and disturbing subject matter.

I am profoundly indebted to Professor Verónica Salter of the Faculty of Psychology and Social Sciences at the University of the West Indies, Mona, Jamaica; Professor Peggy Brooks of the Department of Psychology at the Massachusetts College of Liberal Arts in the USA; award-winning Jamaican-Canadian author Horane Smith; K.Sean Harris, Managing Editor, LMH Publishing Limited; Professor Y. Blagrove Smith, counselling psychologist; Trevor Antonio Francis; Majesty Elohim Tolaka; Miss Yi Yan Zhong and Signorina Claudia Galeazzi. Special thanks to my daughter Daniella Elizabeth Brooks, who provided invaluable help and support as my research assistant. Thanks also to the many others, too numerous to mention here.

INTRODUCTION

Psychology, psychotherapy and the wide range of mental and psycho-emotional problems are mysterious and fascinating to many. Because we readily associate such areas with the forbidden, we tend to keep our distance.

However, most of us later become aware of the extra-ordinary ability of the mind to perplex and amaze us with its astonishing and incredible capacities which are not bound by any physical limitations, space nor time. So whenever this complex mechanism behaves in unexpected or uncharacteristic ways, we become apprehensive, confused and scared.

We instinctively believe that there is a common thread of similitude invisibly linking us all to each other, both at the mental and emotional levels. Therefore, any obvious derangement in the mind's usual function would most naturally imbue us with fear and anxiety.

Furthermore, the widespread misconceptions and falsehoods regarding mental health, and the many modalities of maladaptive behaviour that increasingly manifest in our modern society demand a new approach. Honesty in the dissemination of information about mental disorders, as well as their assessment, analysis, and the current therapies applied in treating them are crucial.

One of the foremost issues facing people who have a mental illness is the prejudice that society holds against them, resulting in stereotypes and negative attitudes. A mental disorder, like anything that is unusual or strange, can make us feel uncomfortable or fearful.

Barbaric and primitive methods were standard forms of 'treatment' employed in numerous psychiatric hospitals and other institutions for the mentally ill, as recently as the mid-twentieth century.

Fortunately, we have come a long way from the dark days when mental disorders were considered the handiwork of The Devil and other evil entities, and it was believed that those afflicted with these conditions were demonically possessed and in need of exorcism or flagellation.

But despite an increase in knowledge of the cause of mental disorders, many persons are still ignorant of the treatment involved in psychotherapy and other psychological methods.

In over three decades, during which I have been involved in the academic field, training counsellors and therapists and doing clinical research, I have become aware of the misinformed views held by many persons.

In addition to a false idea about what takes place in a therapist's office, there are many misconceptions about the work of a psychotherapist in the public domain.

That is why I decided to chronicle, with minimum jargon, some of the most interesting, challenging and thought-provoking cases in the field of abnormal psychology I had the opportunity to work on.

To this end, I chose to fully immerse myself into the mental life of my patients, thereby gaining a sophisticated and profound understanding of their anguish. I was then able to appreciate the many facets and subtle nuances of their psycho-emotional distress and better understand the traumatic experiences they had endured.

My chosen style of narrative non-fiction may be perceived by some as crude and at times emotionally harsh in its portrayal of the human condition. I make no apologies for that, nor for the occasional inclusion of my views as they relate to the issues and personalities presented.

I hope that my effort to open a window into what is perhaps the most misunderstood of all the healing sciences will help to dispel some of the myths and mystery that surround the fields of psychology, psychotherapy and psychological counselling.

The facts of each case, as well as the historical and situational framework in which they happened, are presented as accurately as possible. For obvious reasons though, the identities of clients have been altered or masked. Every effort has been made to protect the dignity of all persons mentioned within these pages.

Miguel F. Brooks
January, 2010
Jamaica, West Indies

Part One
THE JOURNEY

CHAPTER ONE

The Venezuelan Cattle Ranchers

"For of this sort are they which creep into houses, and lead captive silly women laden with sins, led away with divers lusts."

II Timothy 3:6

"At ten o'clock we're going to meet with Omar Pulido Rodríguez and his fiancée. We'll need to gather extensive background data, particularly about the fiancée. She seems to be the one presenting the prominent maladaptive features requiring analysis and treatment. Room 6 would be best," said Dr. Jesús Hernández in a calm and measured tone.

Dr. Hernández always gave me the confidence I needed when dealing with the many challenging situations I regularly encountered in my clinical work at the Mental Health Centre at the Hospital Psiquiátrico de Bárbula in Valencia, Venezuela's third largest city.

I really enjoyed working with Dr. Hernández. He was an outstanding professional and a great teacher with an uncanny ability to convey complex concepts and technical protocols in easily understandable terms. His lessons were often laced with anecdotes and references to his extensive experience in psycho-pathology.

At that time, I was doing a practicum (or internship) at the Hospital Psiquiátrico de Bárbula. I had successfully concluded my studies and training at university and was a candidate for the Licentiate in Psychological Sciences degree.

Omar and Abigail had been sitting in the anteroom for about ten minutes while Dr. Hernández and I studiously observed them through a large one-way glass which gave them a mirror on their side. From inside the office, we had a clear view of them and the entire room.

Being alone by themselves, unaware that they were under observation, their behaviour and mannerisms flowed naturally. The anteroom was outfitted with lush plants, soft colours and background music to relax the minds of the clients, even before the therapeutic session began.

Abigail Vergara was a strikingly beautiful young woman with a petite and slender frame. She had large, expressive eyes and her milky white complexion contrasted with her long, flowing jet black hair. At twenty-two years, she seemed more like a teenager than a woman.

Omar and Abigail were standing side by side, intently looking at a large portrait on the wall. While holding hands, they occasion-ally spoke to each other in hushed tones. They looked like a devoted couple.

Omar, a seasoned modern dancer, had a muscular and well proportioned body. A man of Mediterranean ancestry, he had finely chiselled facial lines, dreamy eyes and a sharp and agile mind.

He and Abigail had aristocratic roots and were heirs to wealth passed down through generations as far back as the Spanish colonial empire and the Bolivarian Republican Era.

Having reviewed the basic information form they had completed, Dr. Hernández asked Omar to come in first, after politely letting Abigail know that she'd be alone for only a few minutes. But what we expected to be a brief interval of preliminary data-gathering with Omar stretched out for more than half an hour. What Omar Pulido told us was riveting.

✿

It had all happened about five weeks before our session, a few days after they had announced their engagement to family and friends at a small gathering at the Vergaras' hacienda, the extensive cattle ranch and breeding station they owned at *El Tocuyo,* on the outskirts of Valencia.

Omar said he had just returned from a business trip to the capital, Caracas, and was eager to give Abigail the little gift and the flowers he had brought for her. He wanted to surprise her. After parking his car beside a clump of trees a short distance from the main house, he entered and asked Domitila, Abigail's faithful long-serving nanny-turned-helper, where she was. She told him that Abigail was at the stables tending to her horses.

As he approached the long brightly coloured structure which housed at least eight horses at a time, he noticed that none of the workers were around. As he slowly and silently entered the dim and smelly paddock through a side entrance, he expected her to be startled upon seeing him. But it was he that was in for a surprise.

We listened in silence as he he told us how shocked he was by what met his eyes: his darling Abigail was on her knees, beneath one of the horses, lustily sucking the beast's enormous genitals. Omar said his heart began to pound rapidly and a feeling of disbelief overtook him. That's all he remembered.

The knotted lump in his throat and the discomforting sensation in his stomach quickly subsided and was replaced by cold sweat and anger, which he automatically tried to control with deep breaths and yoga-inspired self-calming techniques.

By this time he had shifted his position slightly to get a better view of the gross activity his beloved Abigail was carrying out right before his startled eyes. Suddenly, he became aroused. He described the feeling as a creeping and erotic warmth radiating throughout his body, before settling and swelling in his loins.

As Omar was about to continue his shocking narrative, Dr. Hernández interjected with a question: "Did you at that moment notice or become aware of any further signs of your own arousal?"

"Yes, I did, and that was a real surprise for me. I was indeed becoming aroused, almost against my will. It was sort of… unexpected. But at that time I did not pay much attention to it. I was really in a very confused state. I mean, my mind was so confused… so mixed up," Omar replied.

He said the skill Abigail demonstrated with the horse, coupled with the animal's response to her stimulation, forced him to conclude that she regularly indulged in the perverted activity.

Omar said that as he was about to shout and reveal himself, the horse ejaculated, filling Abigail's mouth and then spilling and splashing onto her clothes. Abigail gagged.

Pulling herself away from the animal, still unaware of Omar's presence, she stumbled then leaned dejectedly over the dividing metal rail and began to weep uncontrollably while wiping away the slimy wetness from the front of her blouse with a towel.

He further explained that those images never left his mind since that day and that he started to see Abigail differently. Still, he was very much in love with her.

Sitting before us, Omar leaned forward, stooped his shoulders and clasped his hands. For a tall and athletic young man, he appeared smaller, as if burdened by an invisible weight on his shoulders.

"When I saw her crying like that I felt something move within me, deep in my bowels. My heart just went out to her. I truly felt sorry for her, so I didn't shout. I just softly called her name as I walked towards her," Omar said. "I remember hugging her from behind and constantly saying *Está bien…está bien chica, yo te amo siempre, ocurra lo que ocurra.* It's okay, it's okay darling. I will always love you, no matter what happens.'"

He said he took off his jacket and placed it across her shoulders as they walked home in silence. Though Abigail sobbed softly, they did not speak but pretended that everything was okay. According to Omar, it would have been difficult and emotionally taxing to discuss what had happened.

"It wasn't until four days ago that we talked about it briefly. The conversation came about because she kept asking over and over: 'Do you love me? Do you love me?'" Omar noted. "I even asked her if I had ever given her reasons to doubt my love and commitment. 'We are getting married soon, remember?' I said to her. It was then that she just abruptly said to me, 'I hate it. I just hate it. I really hated doing it, but it's like I can't stop myself from doing it. I am sorry, Omar. I know that I hurt you so bad, but truly, I am sorry.'"

Omar said it was at that point they decided to seek help. He believed Abigail was in need of urgent attention as she had become distressed, worried and increasingly ashamed of what she had done. Omar leaned back in his chair, looked at us rather sadly, and after a while said, "Please, Doctor, tell me the truth. Do you think that Abigail can be helped with that problem?"

❖

To this day, I distinctly remember the recommendation that Doctora Isaura Lobo, one of our distinguished professors, had made during one of her lectures in Abnormal Psychology. She was specifically describing the essential and diagnostic features of various sexual paraphilias, those recurrent, intense and sexually arousing deviant urges and fantasies usually involving non-human objects or animals, which often cause significant distress and mental and emotional anguish in affected persons.

Professor Lobo had urged us to view the Argentinean film *Fuego* which gives an excellent depiction of nymphomania, a sexual disorder of which many popular myths, misunderstandings and downright falsehoods abound.

Nymphomania has traditionally fuelled the frenzied imagination and fantasies of many writers, poets, thinkers and historians and has even kindled a kind of unknown and atavistic fear of the 'devouring female' that lies within the dark recesses of man's subconscious mind.

Known in classical medical literature as 'furor femininus', throughout Latin America as 'fuego uterino' (womb fire), and as a 'white-liver woman' in Afro-Caribbean countries, this profoundly disturbing condition manifests in females as an uncontrollable and insatiable appetite for sexual intercourse.

A form of this affliction in males is known as satyriasis (or the practices of the male satyr or 'Don Juan', the incorrigible seducer, who is nevertheless grudgingly admired and widely celebrated both in the arts and in the popular tales of many cultures).

A few months later, I saw the movie advertised in the press. It was showing at a tacky, rundown cinema in one of the rough neighbourhoods of Valencia, and I decided to go and see it. That turned out to be quite an unforgettable experience. As I sat in the darkened theatre, some rowdy fellow at the rear threw something forward that happened to fall right on my head. I swiftly, in a reflex motion, brushed it to the floor at my feet.

I quickly took out my penlight to see what it was and realized that it was a snake. Immediately I thought it was an imitation rubber-toy snake until I noticed that it started moving slowly. Frightened and almost in panic, I jumped on my seat and yelled '*Culebra, culebra*!' (Snake...snake!)

The fellow sitting next to me looked at it and just casually said, 'Oh, come on, it's just a little river snake.' He then leaned over, grabbed the snake and casually hurled it ahead to the front seats. We then heard some unfortunate soul scream out and loudly curse a string of obscenities in Spanish. I regained my composure, took my seat and hoped that nothing else would happen that evening.

Fuego turned out to be an exceptional movie based on a true story. Starring the voluptuous Argentinean actress Isabel Sarli and Armando Bo, who also produced and directed the film, it vividly shares the story of Beatriz, the beautiful wife of a noted industrialist in Buenos Aires, who was truly and deeply in love with her husband but was also afflicted with nymphomania.

Through Sarli's dramatic and realistic portrayal, one could easily appreciate the anguish and despair of Beatriz as she valiantly struggled with the vice-like grip of the unquenchable fires that seemed to rage in her entrails and which demanded the temporary relief of wild and indiscriminate coitus.

She was increasingly at the mercy of the sick desires that compelled her to seek out that fleetingly elusive orgasmic plateau with any and every available man, as soon as her husband was not around —- be it the delivery men, the store attendant, the casual passer-by.

Her increasingly bold and risky forays in search of casual sexual encounters with total strangers could not remain secret for long, as she had even resorted to suddenly and unexpectedly exhibiting her nude body to strange men who would at times flee from her, obviously startled, and suspecting that she was insane.

Inevitably, Beatriz's husband would learn the painful truth regarding his wife. But their sincere and abiding love prevailed over the disillusionment, anger and shame that enveloped their lives, threatening to destroy their still young and childless marriage.

Their search for a cure, or for some relief to her condition, had taken them to several of the most eminent specialists in Argentina and then to the great metropolitan centres of New York, Paris, Rome and wherever they could find someone who would offer a solution. Beatriz had become severely depressed and frequently contemplated suicide. But a cure seemed to elude them because following periods of normalcy, she would often relapse.

After extended psychoanalysis and various forms of hypno-therapy and mental regression techniques, the origins of her sexual compulsion were traced to childhood abusive traumas, which though repressed, were now fuelling her nymphomania.

In the end, Beatriz came to terms with her abnormal sexual behaviour, but only after confronting and exorcising the psycho-emotional demons of prolonged early sexual abuse. But even after settling down to the domesticity of married life, she occasionally felt the 'call of the flesh', bidding her to return to the intoxicating vertigo of her hypersexual addiction of yesteryear.

❁

We often come across anecdotal references to modern day cases of bestiality, or zoophilia, as it is scientifically termed in Abnormal Psychology. These are the human-animal sexual interactions found not only among horny male youths (who would at times copulate with domestic animals) in rural or agri-cultural settings, but even more so with the sophisticated and wealthy Californian socialites who are known to keep dogs or horses as lovers, many times excluding their human lovers.

To this end, we dealt with a large number of tragic and rare cases at the University Health Centre in Valencia. Some were related to consequential incidents of human rabies, or hydrophobia, as it is properly known, which was fairly widespread in many parts of Venezuela. Others were due to the persistent maladaptive and unusual behaviour of some folks.

Rabies is a fulminating and acute infectious disease of warm-blooded mammals, especially the carnivorous type. Some wildlife, including foxes, raccoons, squirrels, bats and skunks are known to be carriers of the disease, which is caused by the Lyssa group of viruses. The domestic animals which are most susceptible to it are dogs, cats, and even cattle. The disease is transmitted to humans through the bite and saliva of a rabid animal, and it affects the central nervous system causing paralysis and inevitably death. It is an excruciatingly painful disease from which survival is rare. Even the standard treatment is extremely painful, as it requires the administration of a series of rabies vaccine injections, usually lasting a month.

Our colleague and friend, the noted physician Dr. Juán Vicente Seijas, had referred to us the distraught daughter of a fatal rabies victim for grief counselling. The circumstances of her mother's infection with rabies were truly most unusual and were the subject of several reports in the local press.

According to the story, one evening when the victim's young grandson was returning home from school, a dog, later found to be rabid, attacked the boy but only managed to slightly tear the youth's pants cuff. At home, the grandmother stitched and repaired the torn garment but had apparently pricked her finger while doing so and unknowingly introduced a microscopic particle of the infected dog's saliva into her wound. That was enough to start the fatal disease's incubation period. Unfortunately, the initial symptoms were not immediately recognized and remained untreated. She suffered a painful death some weeks after because though treatment had already been instituted, it was too late.

I remember how the public health authorities immediately carried out a massive campaign in Valencia and throughout the Venezuelan state of Carabobo, where they euthanized every dog in sight. Teams of workers, armed with spray guns, went about wetting dogs with the ice-cold poisonous liquid which the animals immediately started licking. They violently convulsed and died shortly after.

Even dogs within the confines of fenced or walled yards were sprayed if seen. Zealous citizens illegally obtained capsules of the deadly substance strychnine to lace meat that was indiscriminately thrown about for stray dogs to consume.

These anti-rabies campaigns periodically took place in selected geographical areas, but the deadly virus still persists in Venezuela. In the hinterlands and deep jungles, rabies is hosted in various mammals which eventually contaminate their domestic cousins in towns and cities.

○

Another incident that really shook us up was a tragic episode involving a young high school student, a brilliant young teenager, who was brought in by the authorities because he showed signs of major depressive disorder. He was also deemed suicidal. The young man, Alfonso Carvajal, was being held responsible for the death of his girlfriend; however, the details were absolutely mind-boggling and heart-rending to say the least.

Carvajal was the son of a veterinary surgeon based near the city of Maracay, in the adjoining state of Aragua, not far from Valencia. He had gotten hold of some yohimbina tablets, which are used to stimulate copulation in cattle. Made from extracts of the bark of the yohimbe, an African tree, the tablets are placed in the animal's drinking water and are considered very effective.

While at a drive-in cinema with the young lady, Carvajal dropped not one but two of these powerful aphrodisiac tablets into the girl's drink. Shortly after consuming some of the liquid, she went into a state of heightened sexual excitation.

They were petting heavily in the semi-darkness in the front seat of the car, when, in her state of hyper-arousal, she sat on the vehicle's gear-stick, which entered her vagina before going deep into her bowels and rupturing delicate internal organs, causing massive haemorrhage. The young lady later died of shock and circulatory collapse even before arriving at the hospital's emergency room.

Cases like these were being dealt with when Omar and Abigail had come in, and though their situation was not as urgent or emotion-laden as the others, Dr. Hernández and his assistants nevertheless gave them the full attention and care that they deserved and expected.

❂

A week after we sat down with Omar, we had an assessment session with Abigail. We saw her alone to establish a rapport with her, a vital prerequisite for a successful intervention.

"Have you ever been to a psychiatrist or a psychologist, or have you ever been psychoanalyzed?" Dr. Hernández asked Abigail calmly, his eyes locked unto hers.

Because he had an unhurried and inviting style, only the initiated would know that he was attempting to disarm Abigail's ego through a popular psychological technique.

"No, Doctor. I've never been," Abigail replied shyly. I wondered if she was using her normal speaking voice. But then

I realised that the unfamiliar surroundings and possibly some degree of intimidation might have accounted for her obvious shyness.

"Well, Abigail, let me explain. First of all, whatever transpires here between us is strictly confidential; it is secret," Dr. Hernandez explained. "No one will ever know. And I mean *no one*. There needs to be total trust between us. Right?"

"Yes, Doctor, I understand," Abigail responded with a smile that danced briefly on her lips.

"Also, as you probably know, our orientation is a bit different from the standard medical perspective which seeks an immediate alleviation of symptoms and physical distress," Dr. Hernandez explained. "In the psychological approach, we endeavour to discover the cause of the problem in order to confront it and obliterate it; even if not completely, then at least, to some extent, that would allow the person to function and be able to cope with the demands of daily living," he added.

He further explained that the techniques would yield results gradually.

"So, Abigail, are you willing to go along with all that and follow our instructions diligently?" Dr. Hernández asked.

"Oh yes, Doctor. I will. I certainly will," she promptly replied.

"Then we will help you. We will do whatever we can to the best of our ability to assist you and Omar, and with your cooperation we'll surely be successful."

Dr. Hernandez then informed her that it would be essential for her to disclose everything in full detail for a proper assessment to be made. Abigail nodded in agreement. But could she really get rid of a condition that had now become a part of her? And did she really want to?

Being the only daughter of Don Nicanor and Doña Rosita, Abigail grew up accustomed to having total privacy in her personal life. Much of her childhood was spent in the company of dolls and toys. Then came her ninth birthday party. She remembered that birthday most vividly because that's when everything changed.

❁

On the morning of her birthday, after her parents had showered her with gifts, kisses and best wishes, Abigail went downstairs to watch the helpers complete preparations for her afternoon party. When she became bored, she decided to go to the stables where Alfio would be. Everyone in the state of Carabobo knew that Alfio Giuffrida was also Doña Rosita's lover. They also knew that Rosita's husband, Don Nicanor, was well aware of it but didn't seem to mind at all. He was busy with the young mistress he kept ensconced at the luxurious apartments he had set up in Valencia.

Alfio, who originally hailed from Italy, had been the competent administrator of the Vergaras' *hacienda* for the last eight years. He had become an asset to the family because of his efficient handling of the sprawling estate and its very profitable cattle and horse-breeding programmes. To Abigail, Alfio was the loving father figure and friend she didn't find in her aloof and often absent dad. Alfio was a confidant who listened to her and was always on her side no matter what. They shared many secrets.

When Abigail reached the stable, Alfio was about to ride out on one of the horses. Seeing him, she jumped and waved her hands excitedly to get his attention. He rode over to her.

"Alfio, I wanted you to saddle my horse for me, but you are going away," she said, pouting and pretending to be annoyed.

"Ah, Chiquitina, I am a bit late, and I have to check the eastern fences now. You can come along with me. Here, let me help you," he said, lifting her onto the horse's saddle.

"Today is my birthday, Alfio," she announced triumphantly, settling her small frame onto the saddle and leaning against Alfio's comfortable chest.

"Oh, wonderful! Congratulations, Abigail. Well, tell me, how old are you now?" he asked, though he already knew her age.

"Don't you know? Yes, you know. I am nine years old, and I will be ten my next birthday," she replied.

"Well, you are a big girl now, so you really have to get serious with your school work. Study hard and read a lot, and you will be okay," he told her.

She reminded him of her mother; they were both beautiful with strong facial lines. But while Doña Rosita had lost much of her beauty to age – she was in her mid-forties – Abigail's was fresh. Alfio often wondered if Abigail knew of his affair with her mother, since Rosita made no effort to conceal it.

They returned to the stables sometime in the afternoon after a rustic but hearty open-fire lunch in the *potrero,* the cattle's grazing flatlands. Before returning, they had assisted with the delivery of a calf and swam in the calm river that runs through a section of the property.

Abigail cherished those moments she shared with the workers on the property, among the livestock and the lush vegetation. Though she had been on such expeditions with Alfio and the farmhands many times before, things were different this time. She felt like somebody else. She felt like she was somewhere else, somewhere new. She felt like Time had stopped for her alone.

"Have you any idea how long that feeling of unreality lasted?" Dr. Hernandez asked.

Knitting her eyebrows, closing her eyes and clasping her hands nervously, Abigail made a desperate attempt to remember, but she couldn't.

"Doctor, that was a very long time ago…I was only nine at the time," she responded.

"Well, okay. Have you ever had dreams depicting anything that happened on that day, on your birthday?"

"Oh yes, Doctor. I dream often, but I don't remember most of the dreams. I remember a dream I had about two months ago. It was about the birthday party. I was cutting the cake with my cousin Ramon, and the cake started bleeding. Then it was no longer a cake, but a bird, a dead bird right there on the table," Abigail said.

"In the dream, were you frightened when you saw the bird there bleeding? And when you woke up, how did you feel about that dream?" Dr. Hernandez asked.

"No, I wasn't scared at all in the dream, and when I woke up I was more amused and curious than anything else. I even told Domitila about the dream, and all she said was that it wasn't a good dream, but she couldn't explain why."

"What about the birthday party? Tell me what you recall about the party. Who was there? What happened? Try to bring a picture of that day into your mind. Try to see everything again, in colours, just as it was on that day. Also try to remember the smells around, like the smell of the food and the people who were there, their lotions and their perfumes. Anything at all."

We remained silent for about four minutes to allow her to connect and reconnect associations in her mind so that they would help her remember that day some fourteen years ago.

Abigail was in a state of equipoise, relaxed and introspective and seated with eyes closed. I had momentarily shifted my attention from her to glance at some scribbled notes on my writing pad, when she suddenly burst into tears, moaning and sobbing uncontrollably.

I immediately went over to her and started taking her through various relaxation procedures, beginning with rhythmic breathing, systematic desensitization and guided imagery, while reassuring and comforting her.

"It's okay, Abigail. It's okay to cry. Now, take in a deep breath…good…let it out slowly. Again, let it out slowly… very good. Again…in…slowly out…good, just keep it like that…and… relax."

I decided to continue with this technique.

"Okay, now look straight out ahead, into open space… and a little above. You are looking far, far away…as far as you can…yes…pass the moon, the sun…the stars…you are floating away… far away, to a very distant point out there…and you feel so light…as light as a balloon…Yes, it feels so nice out there...total silence…it's only my voice you hear now," I instructed her. "You are just floating away…so fast…and far. Yes…very far away you can see a small circle…very small, and you are moving towards it… That little circle is getting slightly bigger… yes…slowly getting bigger…yes, it's a big blue circle now, very big, like the sun…and it is *your* blue circle, Abigail…keep it right there…right in front of you…don't let it move…hold it right before you…breathe in…out… and relax…good. Now tell me, Abigail, what is your horse's name?" I asked almost in a whisper.

After a while, she eventually replied, "I own four horses. Which one of them, Doctor?"

"Your favourite one, Abigail. The one Omar saw you with in the stables."

"I want to stop, Doctor. I really want to stop, but it is not easy because I always feel like something is pulling me. It is so strong, so irresistible, and I just do it again," Abigail responded, avoiding my question.

"We will help you, Abigail. We will work with you. It won't be easy, but don't worry. If you are really determined and diligently follow the methodology and instructions, then I feel certain that you'll be victorious. *We* will be victorious," I said. "Now, can you remember the first time you started doing it? How long ago was it? How did it happen? I want you to describe it in detail. Everything. Take your time and keep your eyes on my moving finger."

"Well, Doctor, I remember it happened right there inside the stables. At the time I was ten years old. Alfio and I were setting some oats and corn for a few of the horses when he started rubbing the horse's belly. He called me over and said that I must also rub the horse. He was smiling. He was always smiling. He said the horse loves when you rub his belly and that it will keep him docile and obedient. Then he showed me how to masturbate the horse. He held my hands and showed me, and I just did it naturally," said Abigail.

"What was going through your mind at that moment? How did you feel about it?" I asked during the brief interlude of silence that followed.

"It was kind of new for me. Even though I had seen the animals mating before, I didn't know that they could also be masturbated. I wondered how the horse felt, but then I saw that he was enjoying it. I became very excited and curious about the whole thing," she said. "Alfio said that I did it very well and that I am a fast learner, so I felt good. I was happy that Alfio showed me how to do it; he's an expert on horses, and I was always eager to please him. He told me not to let anyone know about it because they wouldn't understand. It was our secret."

While speaking, Abigail tracked my finger which I was rhythmically moving across her line of sight. I was using eye movement desensitization and reprocessing (EMDR), a procedure that allows the individual to focus on a traumatic memory while also concentrating on the therapist's moving finger. These dual-attention tasks tend to speed up the mental processing of disturbing material. When the person recalls the disturbing images while moving the eyes, his thoughts become less upsetting, and it's easier for him to think rationally.

"Did you start sucking the horse on that first occasion when Alfio was at the stables with you?" I asked.

"No, I didn't do it to the horse at that time...but...but...Doctor, I knew about it already. I mean, I had done it a few times before... not with the horse...I..."

Abigail's voice trailed off into silence. I did not press her, realising she had dug up memories that were previously repressed.

"Doctor, please excuse me. I need to go to the restroom," she said.

"Certainly. I'll ask a nurse to assist you," I said.

When she returned, we gave her some relaxation and visualization exercises to practise at home. We agreed to meet early for the next therapy session.

○

Later that week we had a session with Omar Pulido. He was in high spirits.

"I am feeling much better, Doctor, mainly because I have noticed a bit of improvement in Abigail. She doesn't seem so sad and moody these days. We really appreciate the help that you're giving her," he said.

"How is the interaction between you two coming on?" I asked.

"Well, that is quite okay, Doc. We're in love, so we should be able to survive this crisis. As they say, love conquers all. We'll be married in April next year, less than six months time, so we need to get this whole affair behind us," Omar said. "Abigail and I get along beautifully. We have a great relationship in every way. So far this is the only problem that we have encountered. Doc, I don't think she will do it again. She is truly sorry and she promised me that she will never do it again."

Omar seemed a bit naive to us. He didn't understand the depth and complexity of Abigail's condition nor the comprehensive therapeutic intervention that was necessary to treat it. It seemed that he, too, was in need of significant cognitive restructuring. He seemed to be grappling with conflicting emotions and disturbing thoughts which he tried to explain. But it was all ego defence mechanisms. Despite the composure and emotional strength he tried to project during the session, we knew Abigail's condition was having a marked effect on him. So, after going through some routine preliminaries with him, I explored aspects of his clinical presentation.

"Omar, we need to revisit the events of that day at the Vergaras' *hacienda* just to elucidate some relevant points and to ensure that they do not become problematic in the future," I explained, noting his attentiveness. "You said that after the incident at the stables you put your jacket on Abigail and walked her back to the house. What was going through your mind at the time?" I asked while scribbling on my writing pad.

"I couldn't think straight at all; I kept smelling the scent of the horse's sperm which was all over the front of her blouse. The scent was very strong like freshly cut grass. I can't forget it," he explained.

"Well, surely that confirms one of psychology's provocative tenets: smells remain almost permanently imprinted in our long-term memory," I said. "What is important here though, are your feelings, your thoughts and emotions. Try to recall, as much as possible, exactly what you felt and thought about at the time."

Omar said he remembered thinking about Abigail's incredible skill at performing oral sex whenever they made love. But so as not to upset or offend her, he never inquired about the source of her expertise. On two occasions, during sex, Abigail had paced her coital movements so well that it brought Omar to the brink of ejaculation. She then inserted a finger into his anus, bringing him to an explosive and immensely pleasurable orgasm. While he enjoyed the experience, he said he couldn't shake the feeling of guilt that lingered; he worried that he was silently harbouring homosexual tendencies.

The anal technique Abigail had used on Omar was a well-known French bordello technique called postillionage, but recalling the episode had made Omar anxious and agitated. We then proceeded to help him examine and come to terms with the thoughts that were troubling him.

○

During one of our regular staff meetings with Dr. Hernández to discuss the cases we were dealing with at the Centre, we agreed to apply a modified version of exposure and response prevention (ERP) and other procedures to Abigail's situation. ERP is a therapeutic approach which would require that she temporarily leave the familiar environment of the animals for a specific period of time. In Abigail's case, she could go spend time with relatives and friends in the city.

Thereafter, she would, under controlled circumstances, be brought back into close proximity to the beasts but prevented from indulging her compulsion. The objective of this technique was to gradually eliminate her obsessive-compulsive behaviour for her to return to a normal and healthy mental state. It was only after several ERP sessions that Abigail finally opened up, allowing herself to be hypnotically guided and immersed into aspects of her relatively distant past. Those were past experiences that she had repressed because they were in conflict with her moral principles.

In her youthful, carefree days, growing up in the idyllic semi-rural surroundings at the *hacienda*, Abigail fell under Alfio's insidious influence. He had taken advantage of the child's innocence and trust, and had deviously introduced her to a wide array of sexual activities for a long period of time.

As she gradually revealed, first in disjointed bits and pieces, then in coherent and detailed narrative, Alfio had been cunningly subjecting her to a series of abusive sexual acts for nearly four years, starting on her ninth birthday. He even pimped her out to some of his friends. It had ended because he left his job at the *hacienda* for another posting in the remote, oil-rich state of Zulia, near to the Colombian-Venezuelan border.

Throughout the therapeutic intervention, which lasted for about eleven months, we had to exercise great care in helping Abigail overcome the profound shame and guilt she constantly struggled with. We concluded that despite her privileged background, Abigail lacked the support of her parents, particularly from her mother, who was totally unaware of what was happening to her daughter.

As we guided Abigail into confronting those traumatic experiences of her childhood, she gradually realized that she was not to blame for what happened.

In further discussions we had at the time regarding Abigail's case, there were noteworthy contributions from other faculty members, including Dr. Gonzáles Garmendia and Dr. Vicente Pontillo. On one occasion, Dr. Pontillo addressed the clinical team.

"I think we should consider the likelihood that Abigail's OCD (obsessive-compulsive disorder) and zoophilia will evolve into a more acceptable form as she settles into her new role as wife. Perhaps even as a mother. She is young, healthy, vibrant and still learning and adopting new patterns of behaviour and responses," said Dr. Pontillo. "We must also remember that for a woman getting married for the first time, this could constitute the single most important event in her life. It's a milepost with positive effects for a woman's self esteem. It's as significant as having a child," he added.

"But, Dr. Pontillo, are you saying that she will likely grow it out or something of the sort?" a bemused Dr. Garmendia asked.

"Yes, certainly. Either that or she transfers her oral fixation exclusively unto her husband," Dr. Pontillo replied.

"Well, it wouldn't be an oral fixation from the baby stage of normal psychosexual development. In Abigail's case, it is certainly a learned behaviour because she was subjected to lengthy and sustained conditioning by Alfio from as early as nine years old," interjected Dr. Hernández, who, up to that moment, had remained mostly silent.

Dr. Hernández asked Dr. Garmendia if he agreed that Abigail was likely to develop healthier forms of sexual expression thanks to the excitement that comes with married life.

"To be honest, I think that would be harder than castrating a mosquito in mid flight," he quipped. His response had us all in stitches for a while. Shortly after, he continued, "No, I don't agree. The whole matter is a very complex one with some rather unique features which makes her future responses and behaviour hard to predict. First, the whole process of the young girl's sexual conditioning was long-lasting and intense, so much so that she has become a devoted equine fellatrix. We also need to take into account the fact that she was not forced or coerced into doing something she didn't want to do. Instead, she was systematically and precociously sexualized."

Dr. Garmendia went on to explain that Abigail had developed a love for performing oral sex on horses. She had become hooked.

"I think we should continue with the multimodal psycho-therapeutic approach taken so far, as these would foster behaviour change and meaningful patterns of personality functioning. But we would also need to ensure some sustained continuity to the intervention to make certain that she doesn't fall into a relapse," he suggested. "Our principal objective with Abigail's presentation should be to facilitate the development of her intra-psychic structures such as her self-concept and self- esteem as well as interpersonal performance like her capacity for genuine intimacy. It is also very important that Omar be fully involved and supportive of her treatment. I suggest that she come in for sessions at least every two weeks for now," he concluded, making it obvious that he expected us to concur with his opinion. We did.

❁

A few months later, we all received formal invitations to Abigail and Omar's wedding and reception. We were overjoyed and saw it as a professional victory. We felt satisfied.

At the lavish wedding reception, held at a palatial mansion in the upscale residential community of *El Trigal,* after the lovely newlyweds made their triumphant entry amidst the traditional blessing of rice grains poured on their heads, Doña Rosita followed the couple. Suddenly, she slipped on some of the rice grains and fell flat on her bottom. Many persons in attendance saw it as an omen for the young couple.

Some two months later, Omar and Abigail came to visit us. Cheerful and beaming, they were returning from their extended honeymoon in Mérida, high in the Venezuelan Andes Mountains, where they rode the cable car to the summit of Pico Bolívar, the highest mountain peak in the country. They said they had a wonderful time.

Omar told us that on the morning after their wedding night, at around seven, the phone in their hotel room rang, and he quickly answered it. It was Abigail's mother, Doña Rosita, asking to speak to her daughter.

"Oh, Doña Rosita, Abigail is still sleeping. She's a bit tired," Omar told her.

"Is she alright ?" Rosita asked with a hint of concern in her voice.

"Certainly, Doña Rosita, she's quite okay," he assured her.

Sitting in our office, Omar and Abigail winked at each other. Then we all cracked up laughing, for we all knew what they were thinking. We certainly knew.

CHAPTER TWO

I Shall Spit upon their Tombs

"For they eat the bread of wickedness, and drink the wine of violence."

Proverbs 4:17

"When you say that this fellow Carlos survived eleven days as a guest of Panama's secret police, I do agree that most likely he is in need of some assistance from us to help him recover from the psychological and emotional impact of such an experience. But I can assure you…well, what I mean is that he can thank his good fortunes that his personal safety didn't become the responsibility of outfits like Venezuela's DISIP [1] or Argentina's ESMA[2], for then he would've known for sure what the term living hell really means," I explained to Norma Llorente, a psychology major. She had been assigned to our unit to complete her practicum. "And, I see here in the data sheet that he wasn't ever in the custody of the Secret Police, but that he was arrested by the G-2, the National Guard's military intelligence section."

Carlos Lernín was a son of Valencia who had recently been deported to Venezuela after an eventful trip to Panama. Glancing through his data sheet, I came across references to terms such as chronic anticipatory anxiety, apprehensive expectation, reality and event distortions as well as sleep disorder, psychomotor agitation, heightened startle response, among others. These are conditions usually associated with victims of torture.

Carlos had been referred to us after he was examined at hospital, and it was concluded that he had been tortured. The clinician who tended to him said he required urgent attention. An appointment was then set up for him, but I insisted that he undergo another medical assessment to be conducted by Dr. Juan Seijas.

It was established protocol at the Centre that all our torture victims were first medically assessed by Dr. Seijas. Dr Seijas was a survivor of brutal torture he endured during his days as a medical student and university student leader during the military dictatorship of General Marcos Pérez Jiménez. He was also very knowledgeable about intense and prolonged torture and the signs of neurological and psychological damage.

❂

For as long as he could remember, Carlos Lernín's life had been a series of crises and disastrous events brought on by his often bizarre behaviour which worried his family. In fact, the troubles began from the day of his birth. Because Carlos was a large baby, weighing over ten pounds, the attending physician had to use obstetric forceps to ease out his large head during the traumatic delivery. But in doing so, the doctor applied too much force to the soft sides of the baby's cranium. This caused some degree of trauma and raised the intracranial pressure in the baby's head.

So when baby Carlos was presented to his mother at the bed-side, she exclaimed, 'No, that is not my baby! Take him away! He's so ugly. I don't want it beside me.' Eventually, however, she reluctantly took the child and lovingly nurtured it.

As a baby, Carlos had bulging eyes like a bullfrog and a hammer-shaped head that gave him a monster-like appearance. But as he grew older, his features gradually changed; he grew handsome and intelligent with an above- average intelligence quotient (IQ). But he also developed disturbing traits in his personality that puzzled his teachers, neighbours and family friends. He was prone to impulsive and unpredictable behaviour; he had a nasty temper and was very unforgiving. He regularly ran away from home, fought at school and stole.

We also learnt that, as a child, Carlos was fascinated with fire and the work of fire-fighters. He wanted to become a fireman. Matches and lighters had to be kept hidden from him due to his unnerving penchant for setting fires. No one knew that at the age of seven, he had been the one responsible for a raging fire that burnt out a large multi-acre pastureland not far from his backyard.

While perusing Carlos Lernín's data sheet, I noticed the pattern of tumultuous events in his life. This alerted me to the possibility that his could be one of those relatively rare cases of anti-social personality disorder (APD), also known as psycho-pathy or sociopathy. But Carlos had never been diagnosed with this particular disorder. Though his behaviour and the disastrous life choices he had made spoke to unusual reality perspectives, he had only recently come to the attention of the authorities in a prominent way.

The salient features and behaviour patterns associated with APD are easy to recognize in affected individuals. Their life trajectory is usually characterized by anomalous crises, broken hearts, ruined friendships, domestic violence, job-related problems, severe marital difficulties, legal and traffic offences, sexual misconduct and promiscuity, and substance abuse. APD usually begins in childhood or early adolescence and progresses into adulthood.

Many affected persons have a history of torturing insects and small animals when they were children, stealing, lying and vandalism, defiance to authority figures and aggression to schoolmates. This baffling disorder poses intriguing and provocative questions, especially from the perspective of psychological research, regarding its cause, possible prevention and treatment. Many affected persons go on to become violent sociopaths as adults.

❂

I was browsing a newspaper and listening to a low-volume morning radio newscast when Maritza Salazar, one of the administrative assistants, knocked softly on my office door.

"Your client is here, sir, but he is more than thirty minutes early," she explained, walking towards the large one-way plate glass between the office and the anteroom, which at that moment was concealed by heavy dark-blue drapes.

She thoughtfully drew away the curtains, uncovering the wall glass. Seated in the room separated from us by the glass barrier was Carlos Lernín. Sharply dressed in business attire, he appeared calm, casually leafing through a magazine. He projected confidence, resembling a successful and progressive young entrepreneur with a promising future. I got the impression that Carlos was deliberately projecting an assured demeanour, offering a likeable alter ego.

The newspaper I was holding carried a story about the capture of a dog that had been trained, allegedly to deflower young girls. Its owner was arrested but was released shortly after due to lack of evidence. In the same newspaper, there was an extensive article on the discovery of the *Agua de Babandí*, an underground spring with marvellous healing properties.

"Sir, are you ready to see Señor Lernín?"

The soft caress of Maritza's angelic voice promptly over-rode the mundane humdrum of my thoughts, bringing me back to the issues that needed immediate attention.

"Oh yes, certainly. Please send him in," I replied.

As usual, before sending in the client, Maritza went across to the large one-way viewing glass and carefully slid back the covering drapes.

"Good morning, Doctor. I am honoured to meet you, sir," said Carlos upon entering my office and settling into a comfortable seat nearby.

"Señor Lernín, on behalf of the faculty and staff here at the Centre, I welcome you and invite you to just relax because this is really a preliminary assessment meeting in which we will try to understand your situation, how you are coping and how to deal with it," I outlined. "We are going to need at least ninety minutes to two hours to go through the whole process," I added.

"That's quite alright, sir. I just wanted to ensure that I did get to see someone here today. That's why I came a bit earlier. I hope that you'll be able to solve my problem, Doc, or rather the multitude of problems I have. I believe they're rather complex," he said while looking at me with an expectant and solemn gaze.

"No, I certainly cannot solve your problem for you, but I can help you to resolve the issues you're facing by offering you a different perspective on those problems, by helping you to understand them and develop suitable coping strategies," I explained.

"No, Doc, no, no. Please, I am sorry, but I don't think my problems are mental or psychological at all. I am convinced of this because, well, I have been observing myself, studying and analyzing all the very unusual things that have been happening in my life, and the direction that my life has taken, especially in recent times," Carlos retorted.

I listened keenly as Carlos spoke while making notes on my writing pad.

"Sir, let me tell you, quite frankly I believe that there is a curse on me. What kind of curse or how it came about or where or who it came from? I have no idea. But as far back in my life as I can remember, Doc, even from childhood days, it's been a constant chain of disastrous and terrible things happening to me. Of course, I recognize that most of them were caused by my own actions and decisions. The choices I made," he admitted. "Hell, I just can't understand why my life didn't go like that of so many other normal, ordinary guys I know. Like all the other people out there who are living ordinary, quiet lives. Mine is just a rollercoaster ride from one crisis to another. It's stressful. I am constantly living on edge, at the edge of disaster, and it is really getting to me, truly."

He added: "Sometimes I even laugh at the pattern of my life. I often stop and wonder what other catastrophe or disastrous calamity lurks around the next corner or the next few hours or days ahead. It is a miracle that I am still alive today. And that's the other thing, too. I would like to know then, what is the purpose of me? I must have been kept alive for one reason or another, despite the many dangerous situations I have put myself in."

In his intense and genuine expression, I could sense an underlying substrate of emotionless and analytical coldness. Perhaps it was in the way he seemed able to detach himself from his emotions and contemplate those troubling happenings in his life as if he were remotely dissociated from them, though inevitably and profoundly affected by them.

"Carlos, tell me, what makes you think a curse is causing your problems and not just the maladaptive, disastrous life choices you've made?" I asked.

"Well, it is just that no matter what I do, where I go or who I associate with, it almost always turns out terribly bad," he replied.

"But surely, there must have been some good times in your life. You have, despite the difficulties you've been through, achieved some measurable success, haven't you? You are a well-educated, intelligent man and a good maintenance engineer with international experience," I pointed out. "Nevertheless, it is very important that you recognize the good things, the positive aspects of your personal achievements so that you can concentrate and build on them, and, in doing so, be grateful for them. Don't you agree?" I asked.

"Oh certainly, Doc. There have been some good periods in my life, but they are usually nullified or neutralized by the disastrous ones that follow, most times soon after. I am really baffled. It is like there is some kind of invisible force operating in me, in full control of my life."

As he spoke, I could see that he was earnestly trying to make sense of the disjointed conundrum his life had become. Carlos went on to outline the succession of shattering and disheartening events that literally threw him into a tailspin and threatened to overwhelm and crush him, although he was no stranger to adversities.

He had been settled and getting along fine in a new job he got in the maintenance and engineering department of a large hotel chain. For eighteen months things had been running quite smoothly there for him, but somehow, deep within, he felt a kind of indeterminate, itchy restlessness he could not pinpoint. It was a disquieting feeling because although he was living alone, but comfortably, in the quarters provided for him at the four star hotel and resort in Isla Margarita on Venezuela's north-eastern coast, somehow he was constantly assailed by the urge to move unto a more exciting and adventurous lifestyle.

It was only when he had the opportunity to meet and fraternize with some of the jet-setting, beautiful people who came to Isla Margarita, the rustically elegant and luxurious playground of the rich and famous, that he indulged, albeit vicariously, in the exciting and ostentatious lifestyle he so admired and longed to be part of.

Carlos met Alfredo Mora and his live-in girlfriend Minerva Echenique Borges, who were vacationing at the resort. Minerva was a Chilean dance instructor and choreographer in her mid-twenties, while Alfredo was a coffee impresario in Panamá. Originally from the Catalán region of Spain, Alfredo had arrived in the Central American isthmus as a child with his immigrant parents and later married into a prominent family.

As Alfredo would later disclose to Carlos, the marriage had greatly helped him to move upwards through the various social rungs of the society. Of course, his Caucasian ethnicity gave him an advantage over the darker skinned locals.

Both men, who were in their thirties at the time, shared similar interests and certain personality traits. Their friendship bloomed. They delighted in reckless, happy-go-lucky and hedonistic thrills, and neither seemed encumbered by burdensome morals or ethics. They soon agreed on plans to meet again, whether in Panamá or right there in Venezuela or wherever their fancy took them.

Being somewhat of a loner, at times appearing shy, Carlos was open to virtually any new experience, any bold and unique adventure, as long as it promised to deliver some exhilarating and joyful stirrings or ecstatic thrill.

Carlos admired how Alfredo was able to fully control his emotions. Alfredo had even confessed to having an open relationship with Minerva, who had been a chronic polysubstance abuser from long before he met her some four years earlier in Panamá, where she worked as a dancer and hostess at one of the capital city's many cabarets. She was a heavy user of marijuana, cocaine, alcohol and tobacco.

Minerva had an intriguing mix of European and Amerindian roots. She was beautiful with full, sensuous lips, a fit and shapely figure and exquisitely smooth olive skin. She was fully aware of the appeal of her distinctive physique and always tried to show it off, whether in a pair of tight-fitting pants that seemed to have been painted on her or in hip-hugging shorts that accentuated the roundness of her buttocks.

As they hung out together, thoroughly enjoying each other's company, crawling around to different discos and bars, then partying and sleeping over in the wee hours of the morning at Carlos' quarters, it soon became quite clear to Carlos that Alfredo was deliberately encouraging a closeness between him and Minerva. Sometimes Alfredo would be conveniently absent for extended periods.

He remembered one morning at breakfast Minerva started playing footsie with him under the table, totally unconcerned about her boyfriend being beside them. When Carlos was forced to look at her in response to her insistent toe-pinching beneath the table, she took a banana from the fruit basket and while staring at him lustily, she slowly began eating the banana in a tantalizing and slow-motion mimic of heavenly fellatio that held him mesmerized.

Minerva displayed an uninhibited and provocative sensuality that was new to Carlos. On many occasions she would pull him unto the dimly lit dance floor to hungrily plaster her body unto his, relentlessly slithering and gliding the silk of her sheer evening gown in childishly mischievous antics of erotic exhibitionism. This never failed to arouse Carlos quickly and visibly.

Initially Carlos would feel uncomfortable with Minerva's openly libidinous ministrations while Alfredo looked on with the curious grin of an experienced, lecherous voyeur. But Carlos soon got over the feeling and gave free reign to his most basic animalistic impulses. Soon enough he and Minerva were having sex regularly, freely and without restraint, with encouragement from Alfredo. Carlos became so engrossed with Minerva's enthusiastic and uninhibited lovemaking that he even took a few sick days off from work to totally submerge himself into the ecstasy of her wild brand of shameless sexual acrobatics.

In narrating these experiences, Carlos closed his eyes and joined his fingertips close to his face in a prayerful gesture, as he relived the intensely erotic encounters when they were at each other "like cannibals in an eating frenzy."

Though he had been strongly impressed by those unforgettable times in Isla Margarita, he felt no true emotional attachment to Minerva, neither to Alfredo; he could easily dispense with them at a moment's notice and not even miss them, for as he saw it, there were many others out there, maybe even better ones. All that mattered was the pleasurable experience he enjoyed, pleasures he could easily replicate at any time with someone else.

After Alfredo and Minerva left for Caracas, where they would spend almost a month, they faithfully kept in touch with Carlos through frequent telephone calls and occasional letters. It was while there, during one of their telephone conversations, that Alfredo invited Carlos to travel with him to Panamá, where he could explore the many business and financial opportunities available there. Alfredo said he would be more than happy to show Carlos around and introduce him to some important and influential people there.

○

I had encouraged Carlos to freely disclose the events and circumstances that led to his traumatic experiences in Panamá. Although he was definitely giving much prominence to his encounter and friendship with Alfredo and Minerva, it was obvious that the real source of his maladaptive behaviour and consequent social problems was his multifaceted personality warp.

There is always reluctance among experienced clinicians and therapists to rush into a premature diagnostic labelling of persons though signs and symptoms seem to fit a specific condition. In complex cases, such as that of Carlos Lernín, the therapist's essential task is to explore both the expressed and the unexpressed elements that emerge in the client-therapist communication.

If sufficiently rigorous analytical skills and some degree of diagnostic suspicion are brought to bear upon the clinically significant data that emerges from this interaction, the therapist can then proceed to conceptualize a working model or a therapeutic approach to apply to the particular client.

By blending his theoretical framework of the client's personality to the therapy process and to the information provided by the client, the therapist is then able to organize the data and make the client's behaviour intelligible. The apparent complexity of this task is easily surpassed by the perspicacity and instinctive, practised skill of an experienced psychotherapist.

Acquiring an insightful schema of an individual's behaviour pattern and the motivation dynamics underpinning those behaviours is of fundamental importance. This is so because early in the therapeutic intervention we need to have an understanding of the client's perception of the world and how he interprets those perceptions. If that perception or its interpretation seems warped or dysfunctional, we then try to find out what caused it to be so.

I was already aware of some of the challenges inherent in Carlos' presentation, particularly the long-standing, pervasive maladaptive difficulties he had been experiencing as a set pattern in his life. And although we design and apply a new therapy for each client according to his or her unique clinical presentation, there were some basic treatment formats we often relied on. Choosing a therapeutic approach depended largely on the psycho-therapist's training, his theoretical orientation and his skill and experience.

In our experience at the Centre, we found Ericksonian hypno-therapy[3] very useful in facilitating change. As long as there is a momentum towards behavioural or attitudinal change, we can always build on it and help bring about salutary and beneficial effects in the client's life. At the time, there was much that Carlos did not reveal to us, maybe for reasons he deemed important. But that is common with clients during early sessions.

❁

Carlos Lernín said he abandoned his job in Isla Margarita and left for Caracas, where he met up with Alfredo, who seemed genuinely happy to see his friend again. They remained in the spectacular Venezuelan capital for a mere three days before going on to the city of Barquisimeto, then onto the oil-rich city of Maracaibo, approaching the Colombian-Venezuelan border region of La Guajira in the northwest coastal area. Sharing the driving duties, they gradually devoured the forty eight-hour drive through the extensive agricultural and cattle-rearing savannah region.

Eventually they arrived in the port city of Barranquilla, located on Colombia's Caribbean coast, where they stayed for four days, awaiting air travel connection to Panamá. While there, they toured the fleshpots of the town, luxuriating in many live sex shows at exclusive night clubs and cabarets. They returned to their hotel with two very attractive young prostitutes, one of whom turned out to be a transvestite, who was so thoroughly feminized that nobody realized that *she* was really a *he* until Alfredo made the discovery while in the throes of ecstasy.

Shortly after arriving in Panama and settling down for a few hours in Minerva's small and cosy apartment in the upscale residential suburb of Punta Paitilla, they went on a tour of the famous Panama Canal, where they marvelled at the huge ships traversing the narrow passageway from one ocean to another. But Alfredo was eager to return to the city; he had promised Carlos a tour of the principal whorehouses of the capital. They visited many of the lurid and dimly lit multi-room houses with colourful names like *Villamor* (Village of Love), *La Gloria* (The Glory), and then racier spots like *El Panty Loco* and *La Casa de los Pantys*, where uninhibited private orgies and multi-partner sexual circuses occurred regularly.

Carlos indulged his lavish sexual compulsions to the hilt, at times paying a prostitute to do uncommon things to her or offering more money for an additional partner, male or female, to join them. He was determined to be more daring each time, inching gradually towards the most bizarre activities.

As he tried and tested every imaginable perversion he had either seen or read about somewhere, he came across a woman named Elizabeth Ramos, who was even more highly sexed and kinky than he was. She willingly matched and even surpassed his appetite for all manner of forbidden sexual pleasures. She was into tight-lacing[4] and sensuous biting, and had been working at the world-famous brothel on Vía España called *La Gruta Azul* (The Blue Cave) for the past three years. A sultry beauty from Nicaragua, barely in her twenties but far more knowl-edgeable than her age suggested, Elizabeth had already had a string of broken and almost tragic relationships peppering her young and tumultuous life.

Initially Carlos was captivated by the haunting depth and focused gaze of her almond-shaped, dark eyes, but he soon became even more enthralled with her almost total lack of inhibitions and the casual way in which she flaunted her sexuality. It bothered him, but just a little, that Elizabeth seemed to have an innate ability to bring out his ugliest animalistic impulses.

He and Elizabeth developed a kind of spontaneous, casual friendship, and on a few occasions they had even been out to dinner or to watch a movie. She also tearfully shared with him aspects of her secret life, including how she first entered the country as a tourist but worked as a prostitute to help provide for her family, which included a crippled brother. Her daughter attended an exclusive private school in Managua, the Nicaraguan capital. Back home, her relatives were under the impression that she had established a variety store in Panama and was engaged in commercial activity there and therefore needed to travel regularly to the isthmus to take care of business.

Caught up in his hedonistic fantasies, Carlos had paid little attention to the state of affairs in Panama at the time. Panama was being ruled by the Guardia Nacional, the militarized police organization that had seized power from a corrupt clique of oligarchs and politicians. But the harsh reality of the situation there, under the so-called 'soft dictatorship' of General Omar Torrijos, became very clear to him one night when he was with Elizabeth, Alfredo and Minerva at a popular nightclub, dancing and having a few drinks.

Just as Elizabeth snapped a second photo of the friends seated at the table, a burly man came out of nowhere, approached them and said, "Sorry lady, you cannot take photos in here."

"But why, what is the problem? We're only taking pictures of ourselves, no one else," Minerva said in an annoyed tone.

Because of the darkness, they could not fully discern the man's physical features.

"Well, my boss, Coronel Hurtado, is here and he does not want any pictures taken. So if you know what's good for you, just make sure that flashbulb doesn't go off again," the man replied before walking off into the darkness.

Alfredo, who had remained quiet, immediately called the waitress, settled the bill, and they all quietly left.

○

One night disaster struck. Carlos was totally unprepared for what happened.

Soon after they dropped Elizabeth and Minerva at a beauty salon, Alfredo realized he had forgotten to bring along some important papers, so he and Carlos had to return to the apartment to fetch the documents. Ten minutes later, as they were driving out through the narrow driveway unto the street, a man emerged from behind the thick shrub, urgently signalling them to stop.

"Alfredo Mora?" he asked while his eyes swiftly searched the car's interior.

"Yes. What is it?" Alfredo asked.

"You are under arrest. G-2, National Guard Military Intelligence."

Even before the man finished his sentence, Carlos noticed that there were at least four other individuals, all in plainclothes and obviously armed, standing a few metres ahead. A car was used to block the entrance.

The man was swiftly joined by another who opened the back door. Both of them then entered the vehicle, loudly cranking their weapons.

"Don't try anything, just follow that car ahead," one of them ordered.

"Hey, what is all this about. It must be some kind of mistake, we haven't done anything wrong. Where are we going?" Alfredo indignantly demanded to know while obediently driving behind the other vehicle.

"Just drive on and everything will be okay. We're heading to the *Comandancia*," the man said.

The *Comandancia* was the military headquarters, a frightening complex that was not strange to Carlos. Two weeks before, he had been there, at the immigration department, where he was granted an extension of his stay in Panamá. But right now he was assailed with intense trepidation and a sense of impending doom, as he had no idea what could have caused his friend to bring down such a calamity upon them both.

As they entered the sprawling compound, located smack in the heart of the downtown slum of El Chorillo, Carlos became aware of a mixture of pungent scents that invaded his nostrils. The wafting smell of garlicky-onion stew was soon replaced by the smell of stale urine, dried vomit and disinfectant.

They were taken to separate sections; Carlos to a small 'office' on the ground floor and Alfredo to some other unknown area. Carlos would not see or hear anything at all from his friend for the next eleven days. Before long, the interrogation began.

"I can't tell you what I know nothing about. I met Alfredo in Venezuela at the hotel I was working at. He invited me to come to Panama, and that's it. I really know nothing about his business or his personal affairs," Carlos frantically explained to the investigator called Lucho, a diminutive for Luis.

It soon became clear to Carlos that he, Alfredo and Minerva, had been under surveillance for months, most likely from the moment they had arrived in Panama. The interrogation was merely to confirm what the authorities had already gathered from telephone wiretaps, mail intervention and tracking. Carlos couldn't believe that all this was happening, but somehow he knew that everything was really real, including the organization's large shield and motto on the wall: G-2 Inteligencia Militar, 'Siempre Alerta' (Always Alert). Beneath, another slogan read 'Por la Razón o por la Fuerza' (By Reason or by Force).

"Sir, I would like to call a lawyer. I know nothing about this matter," Carlos told Lucho.

"What did you say? A lawyer? Hey, you fucking idiot, don't you know who rules in this country? We lock up lawyers in here everyday, and not even your country's embassy can tell us what to do. *We* are the law here, the *only* law," Lucho replied. "Your friend has been moving lots of white stuff[5] for the Mexicans, and now that you have joined his group, you are pretending that you know nothing about it. That whorish woman you're both sharing came back to Panamá three weeks before with a cargo, and then you both followed her. You are staying at her apartment too, and you're telling me that you don't know what is going on? If you know what's good for you, you'd better come clean with me."

Added Lucho: "You won't get out of here alive unless you tell us what you know about the deliveries and financing of the merchandise. As a matter of fact, I am not wasting any more time with you. Hey, Rodrigo! Rodrigo! Come here…take this piece of shit from in front of me! Throw him into the time machine!"

Although Carlos had braced for a variety of outright tortures, it was their creative use of arbitrary threats that was most unnerving to him. His mind was racing through all the terrifying scenarios of being thrown into the time machine as he frantically anticipated what manner of torments awaited him there.

As he recalled the many blood-curdling things he had heard about the techniques often applied by the skilled interrogators serving military dictatorships, he felt the rough grab of pincer-like hands at the back of his neck. His left arm was pulled up to his shoulders, lifting him off the chair.

He could not see who was doing this but merely heard the fellow's grunt at the nape of his neck. He then felt a nauseating pain that radiated from his left shoulder down to the elbow and across the top of his back. He was being pushed from behind, almost trotting at the tip of his toes, through a darkened passage. A sudden stop and a tripping sidekick brought him face down to the floor, only to be quickly lifted to his feet again and roughly kicked at the base of his spine into a pitch-dark cavern.

He heard the loud bang of a heavy metal door behind him almost at the same instant that he crashed unto a rear wall and slowly slid to the ground. Not even the slightest sliver of light shone through a crack, a hole, or even a slender crevice any-where in the cavern. The place was so nauseatingly stink; it reeked of dried faeces and urine.

Seated on the ground with his back to the wall, Carlos became aware of a pulsating pain in his shoulder and neck. Though he tried to ignore it, it soon spread to the base of his skull. Had they just thrown him in there to be forgotten until he starved to death or died of thirst? They certainly seemed to have the power to do whatever they wanted to anyone, at any-time, and anywhere within the territory of the Republic of Panamá. Carlos tried his best to stay calm; he needed to think straight.

Carlos was unaware at the time that he was being subjected to tested modalities of applied psychology, one of which is sensory deprivation or what the interrogator had called the 'time machine'. Being deprived of one's sensory stimulation – not seeing, hearing, smelling, touching – soon bring about distortions in our space and time perception. In other words, the individual is being forced to look inward, thereby embracing his thoughts.

All this makes his most private thoughts more readily accessible to a skilled interrogator using enhanced interrogation techniques, forcing the subject to remain unnaturally bent and twisted into various stress positions while being stringently questioned. Shortly after, the individual would be wracked by excruciating pain caused by the sustained and abnormal stretching of sinews, muscles and tendons, and by traumatic stress on the joints. This invariably makes the victim eager and willing to cooperate in the hope of being rewarded with some relief from his unbearable pain.

After emerging from a fitful sleep, Carlos methodically reviewed and analyzed the events that had preceded his arrest. He could not overcome a subtle but nagging feeling that some-how he and his friends had been betrayed by someone, by a person or persons close to them, who were also aware of Alfredo and Minerva's activities and their contacts.

Just then, he heard the patter of footsteps in the passageway, and he lurched forward in the darkness towards the metal door and banged on it with his elbow. A rough voice on the outside responded, "Hey! What a surprise! My my, one is still alive in there, eh? Ha, ha, ha!" Then the voice disappeared.

Sometime later, as he was about to sink into despair, he again heard sounds on the outside, but this time it was accompanied by the jingle of keys. Then the heavy door opened slightly, allowing a very dim shred of light from a weak bulb in the passage to be faintly seen. A plastic tray and cup were placed on the floor by someone he could not see.

"Hey, what's going on? I want to talk to somebody. When am I getting out of here?" Carlos frantically asked the fellow standing just outside the cell. He then saw another person standing further behind.

"Listen, I am not supposed to talk to you. You are *incomunicado* (in isolation); no one must talk to you, understand? And those are orders from above. Just cooperate and your problem will be resolved soon, ok?" With that, the fellow slammed the heavy door with a deafening bang. The place was totally silent again.

While carefully groping in the dark, Carlos became aware of an intensifying rage growing within him, a seething anger that was begging for a specific target. He sniffed the cold contents of the platter: a piece of hard bread, a bit of lumpy rice with some congealed corned beef on it. He was not hungry, but slowly sipped the cocoa-like liquid in the jug, wondering whether it was breakfast, lunch or supper. He didn't know if it was day or night. He was totally disoriented and in a floating limbo of suspended animation. The so-called 'time machine' had effectively softened Carlos, making him more receptive to suggestions and willing to cooperate with his captors. But surprisingly, he was not subjected to further interrogation. He had remained in total isolation for four days and then transferred from the *Comandancia* to the nearby *Cárcel Modelo* (Ideal Jail), where, after nine days in further isolation, he was suddenly taken to Panama's Tocumen International Airport and deported to his homeland of Venezuela.

✿

On the day of their arrest, Minerva had been speedily picked up at the beauty salon. She was taken to one of the interrogation rooms at the far southern end of the *Comandancia*. She was placed in a cellar, almost subterranean and virtually soundproof, effectively serving its original purpose as a classic torture chamber to be used by the 'specialists', those shadowy and baleful individuals who had been taught macabre and terrifying torture techniques from Cuban, Brazilian, and East German advisors.

Lucho, the experienced investigator with main responsibility for the Carlos/Alfredo/Minerva case, was upset and in a nasty mood after his boss, Manuel Antonio Noriega, had ordered him to complete the investigation and report to him within forty eight hours as more pressing and critical matters had come about. Lucho had realized that Carlos had no new or useful information to provide, so he'd just dismissed him and turned his attention to Minerva, whom he knew would definitely turn out to be a gold mine of valuable intelligence on Alfredo Mora and his international drug connections.

Lucho walked briskly along the corridor and down the short flight of stairs towards the special windowless, bunker-like room, his heart beating rapidly. He was eagerly looking forward to the orgasmic thrills he was about to experience while indulging his most sadistic fantasies. Two other operatives, Melquiades Gómez and a man called 'Cholo', were in the room with Minerva. She was blindfolded and seated at the edge of a rough wooden bunk. There were bruises and blue-black haematomas on her face, shoulders, and legs. Her hands were tied behind her, and she was soaking wet and almost totally naked. Lucho watched with concentrated interest as the blindfolded Minerva rhythmically moved her head up and down Cholo's erect penis.

"Call Atilio, tell him to get here right away. Come on man, move it!" Lucho shouted at a smiling and leering Melquiades, who dashed to the door in obedience to his superior's orders.

Atilio Pulgar and his colleague Cholo were young aboriginal Cuna Indians from the archipelago of San Blás, which spans the north-eastern coast of Panamá. Many of the Indians had been recruited for the country's National Guard and secret police as shock troops, mindless goons who eagerly carried out the instructions of those who fed and clothed them.

Atilio was a retarded petty criminal and a convicted sex offender who Lucho protected and had placed on his team of 'investigators'. His notoriety as a sex pervert with an insatiable appetite for sodomizing his victims was well known. He also had an extremely large penis which he loved to show off. This endeared him to the team.

The minute Atilio entered the room, he fastened his eyes on the hapless Minerva, who still had Cholo's pulsating genitals in her mouth. Seeing the lustful look on Atilio's face, the other men burst into raucous laughter, totally oblivious to their victim's painful groans and moans. They then watched as Atilio undressed and positioned himself behind Minerva. After moistening her anus with some of his tobacco-stained saliva, he proceeded to gradually insert his unbelievably thick organ into her. With each thrust, a scream burst from Minerva's stuffed mouth. She gagged. She coughed. Her eyes filled with tears. But her tormentors just ignored her cries.

Lucho found pleasure in tormenting his victims sexually. He loved to blend his bisexual urges with his obsessions for a uniquely erotic experience. That supreme ability to affect events and someone else's life without being affected, and the ability to cause pain without being touched by it, creates the cognitive and the psycho-emotional conditions that easily encourage sadism, insensitivity, and grandiosity.

The true sadist, an artisan of exquisitely demonic tortures who enjoys inflicting pain, sees torture as a game and the victim as the toy. The ability to taunt and revel in his own invulnerability and compare it to the victim's enslavement are all part of the essence and seductive allure of the brutal craft.

Lucho knew within himself that he had developed a psychological addiction to this rare psycho-sexual stimulus, but he didn't care. He didn't mind as long as he could get to experience it every now and then. He had a deep and strong urge to look into the victim's eyes and see the grotesque facial formations emerging in response to the intense pain they were feeling.

Atilio had almost inserted his enormous organ into Minerva's bowels. Such deep rectal penetration causes vago-vagal shock during which the intense pain surge is instantly and repeatedly felt as it travels up the spinal cord before exploding like a blinding flash of multicoloured lights right in the deep centre fold of the brain.

The pain was so intensely wracking that with each of Atilio's fierce thrusts, Minerva felt as if her eyes were being violently pushed out of their sockets from inside her skull. Then, just as she was about to lose consciousness, Cholo began ejaculating deep down her throat, yelling and shouting in ecstasy.

Minerva passed out shortly after but was quickly revived with a bucket of water thrown in her face. She incoherently babbled to her tormentors that she had told them everything she knew about Alfredo Mora and his operations. She then offered to tell them even more, whatever they wanted to know, whatever they wanted from her.

"Tell us what? We haven't even started to ask you anything yet, and you're offering to tell us? Of course, you're going to talk! I know that for sure. You *will* tell us what you know and also what you don't even know. When I'm finished with you, you're going to wish you weren't born, you bitch!" Lucho shouted angrily at her.

They worked on her mercilessly, alternating the application of a variety of sophisticated and crude methods to invariably inflict excruciating and sustained pain to the most sensitive areas of her anatomy. Electrodes from an Israeli-designed variable trans-former were attached to her nipples, ear lobes, and vaginal lips. One was also inserted into her rectum.

As the surge of high-voltage electricity instantly entered her wet body, her muscle tone flattened and she lost control of her bladder and bowels, which suddenly expelled their contents. She felt as if all her cells had exploded into an uncontrollable paroxysm of convulsions, coursing like a river of hot flames through her rigidly taut body. Her belly seemed to have been blasted to pieces when the electric jolt surged through her.

The torture lasted for about five days and ended because an orderly detected dangerously low levels of arterial blood pressure in Minerva's body. To prevent cardiac collapse, she was rushed to the Hospital Santo Tomás, a short distance from the National Guard's headquarters, where she remained for over ten days.

Months later, while safe at home in Venezuela, Carlos learnt of the terrible circumstances that had befallen his friends. He became suspicious when he learnt that though their acquaintance Elizabeth Ramos had also been arrested, she was released shortly after. They never heard from her again.

○

Throughout the course of many lengthy therapy sessions, Carlos spoke bitterly about his experiences in Panama. He said he was angry and deeply ashamed of what had happened. He had been deported to Venezuela with not even a cent in his pockets. He had only the ragged clothes that he was wearing at the time.

"Doc, I knew nothing about what Alfredo and Minerva were doing. I had no reason to be suspicious of them. There were no signs to suggest that they were involved in drug trafficking. And those officers just grabbed me up, deprived me of my freedom, and subjected me to humiliation and abuse. They even stole everything they could find in the apartment, right down to my clothes, my underwear, and so on," Carlos revealed. "When they realized that I truly had no useful information, they just sent me home with my passport stamped *deportado*, and in those shameful and terrible conditions I was in. I tell you, Doc, even if it is the last thing I do in life, I am going to get even with them. I don't know how or when, but I am really determined to get justice in whatever way possible. I will wait, for somehow I just know that the day and the opportunity will come when I shall spit upon their tombs and have the great joy of standing on the very soil that is covering their wretched carcasses. It shall be my greatest pleasure to urinate on their graves, wherever I may find them," he added.

He spoke with passion and fervour while occasionally tightening his fists. His eyes looked cold.

"Carlos, did you know that harbouring such intense emotions, such deep feelings of rage and pent-up hatred within will make you sick? Grief and envy generate dangerous adrenaline-like substances in your body. We call them psycho-toxins and excito-toxins, but they are really poisons, and once they reach certain levels in your blood and tissues, they interfere with the normal functioning of your body, jeopardizing your health and putting you at serious risk. You have to protect your physical and mental health," I advised him.

We then took Carlos through some basic relaxation procedures involving deep, rhythmic breathing with guided imagery and thought-stopping techniques interspersed with mental blanking. He responded well. But in probing his subconscious mind with the projective techniques of the Rorschak inkblot test[6] and the Thematic Apperception Test[7], among others, we realized that he was struggling with repressed mental distress and psychogenic pain which he had not disclosed or shared with anyone, at least not with us in the clinical setting. Our conclusion was soon confirmed.

"Now, Carlos, those bad memories and experiences in the rear boxes of our minds, we must try to let them remain where they are. There are two things we can do to let them stay there. First, populate the front of your mind with only good and pleasant memories and experiences, the triumphs and sweet moments, the great achievements and good times," I instructed. "Next, you need to take away the emotional component of the experience so that when you recall it, you are not so deeply shaken and distressed by it. Once you extinguish or significantly reduce the emotional impact it has on you, then you can rationally contemplate and better understand the events, their causes and so on. You will have more control over them, which is very important because the memories will always be there."

I then encouraged him to forgive the men who tortured him. Forgiveness has great therapeutic value, especially in bringing about a much-needed catharsis or purging in situations like the one we were dealing with.

He listened with eyes closed and hands placed together as he regularly did. He looked deeply relaxed.

"Forgive? That is not possible, sir. Not after what they did to me. You don't know certain things that happened there. That's why you are saying that I should forgive them. I do agree with all that you said about the negative emotions and the mental poisoning, and I agree that forgiveness is a good thing, but not in this case. It's not possible; I will always want revenge for that...I..." he said, before trailing off.

"Carlos, we know that other disturbing things happened to you in Panamá; things that you have not disclosed to us. But we are here to help, not to judge or condemn. We are your friends. No need to be ashamed. We have seen everything here; nothing surprises us anymore. We are sworn keepers of many secrets."

He did not immediately respond, but after a while, with eyes closed, he began speaking in a low tone.

"I was also raped in there. It is something I am talking about for the first time. Never said it to another soul, but I trust you. It is only my strong desire for revenge that keeps me going. I would not hesitate to bring down an entire nation just to pay them back for what they did to me. Whenever I think about it I start shaking all over and then my head starts aching."

Disclosing his experiences at the *Comandancia* was an unsettling, nerve-wracking exercise for him, but he tried to appear calm and in control of his emotions. Carlos said while he was locked up, he was so receptive to any act of kindness that he willingly accepted a marijuana joint that one of the fellows had offered him, along with a small paper cup containing some kind of juice. It was the same guy who had brought the food on the tray.

He said his name was Melquiades. He befriended Carlos. Speaking to him through the metal door, from the dimly lit passage-way, he encouraged Carlos not to lose hope. He had also told him, and correctly too, that he would soon be taken out of the cell, 'the time machine', and taken to the nearby jail, where he would be better off. But either the drink or the joint had been laced with something. Carlos said he only remembered falling asleep while talking to Melquiades. When he woke up, he realized that he had been sodomized. He felt pain in his rectum and noticed seminal fluid leaking from his anus.

Carlos had regular therapy sessions with us for six months, during which he responded well to treatment and showed good signs of adjustment and some level of cognitive stability. He had not achieved optimal functioning, but he could function adequately as long as he wasn't faced with reminders of the painful events of his past.

We kept in touch, but sometimes we didn't hear from him for months. Nevertheless, he would always resurface, either through a brief phone call, a greeting through a colleague or some other medium. Generally, he seemed to be doing well.

○

In December 1989, The United States government launched Operation Just Cause, a military invasion of Panama. This was great news for the international community. The invasion led to the ousting of Panama's 'tin horn' dictator, Manuel Noriega. At the time, I did not immediately connect these happenings to Carlos Lernín, neither to what I knew about his terrifying experience in Panama. But then I received a telephone call from him, and it quickly brought back all the details of his experiences.

"Hey, Doc, I can't believe this. I just can't believe that it's really happening! That slimy bastard *Cara de Piña* ('Pineapple Face', Noriega's nickname); the Americans are finally frying his balls for good. There he is now, running around and hiding like the coward rat that he is. I wasn't expecting this at all, Doc. This is fantastic! This is great news!" he exclaimed. "I heard on the radio that the National Guard's headquarters, the *Comandancia,* the very building where I was held in that stinking basement, in the 'time machine', has been demolished. I hope those *hijos de puta* (sons of whores) Lucho, Melquiades and all the others were in there at the time. I can just imagine them fleeing in terror and despair. Man, I tell you, God bless America. I'll be coming to see you soon. I'll be celebrating for sure," Carlos said enthusiastically. He had no sympathy for the people of Panama who had suffered an immense tragedy. About three thousand died and countless others were seriously injured.

About ten years after the US invasion of Panama, Carlos was invited to attend a trade conference in the Central American country. He had second thoughts about accepting the invitation, but he later decided to attend the conference and use the opportunity to do some sightseeing. He made no effort to contact Alfredo, Minerva or even Elizabeth on his return.

In the end, the brief return visit to Panama turned out to be anticlimactic. It gave him no real sense of satisfaction. He went to see what was left of El Chorrillo, the rundown neighbourhood where the infamous *Comandancia* was once located. As he stepped out of the vehicle that took him there and strolled through the remains of the former military complex, he felt no victory. Instead, his heart went out to the poor families – the scores of men, women and children – who had died tragically during the bombing. Carlos then realized that he had matured with the years. He had found the strength he had been searching for all his life. He was a changed man.

Then, suddenly, all the memories came rushing back, and the anger, hatred, shame and unquenchable desire for revenge flooded his mind again like waters from a burst dam. Carlos then ceremoniously and very deliberately spat on the dusty ruins at his feet. Three times. He then quietly walked back to the waiting vehicle.

❂

Part Two
THE BECOMING

CHAPTER THREE

The Sanctified Lecher

"Whosoever is born of God does not commit sin, for his seed remains in him, and he cannot sin…"

I John 3:9

Mordechai Brown's mother was an energetic and feisty woman, who was determined to properly raise her five "fatherless" children – three boys and two girls – so that they would survive in the harsh, cutthroat world. Jennifer, or Miss Jen, as she was popularly known throughout the district of Kendal in the rural Jamaican parish of Manchester, was a strong but obstinate country-woman with flawless dark skin and a shapely figure.

She reared goats, chicken and cattle, and sold fruits and vegetables at the local market. She believed strongly in hard work and family, but she was a deeply superstitious woman who cherished her Afro-centric roots. She wore two guard rings and anointed herself daily with several oils and perfumes. And even though she was keenly attracted to various animistic groups with cultish and healing practices adopted from Africa, she had never become a formal member of any group because of her many duties and responsibilities which left her very little time for anything else.

Miss Jen was therefore disappointed when her youngest son, Mordechai, took up religious studies and trained to become a pastor. But she was happy that he had chosen a decent profession and became a respectable man with a nice wife. Her other children were all hustlers in her eyes. And in her moments of anger she would loudly proclaim to all who could hear that the Lord had given her two thieves, two prostitutes, and one upright son. But they were her children, and she would fight and do anything to defend them, no matter what they did. And Miss Jen certainly had to fight for her children. The older boys often had frequent run-ins with the law, and her daughters earned reputations as 'man thieves' and were often involved in noisy brawls with other women over their husbands.

To help solve her problems, Miss Jen regularly visited a popular practitioner of witchcraft, known as an obeahman in Jamaica. His balm yard or spiritual church was located within a sprawling, walled enclosure, smack at the edge of the main road in the mountain district of Mount Rosser in the parish of St Catherine. This obeahman was known across Jamaica, at least by reputation. He allegedly kept a monkey that people said was possessed by the ghost of an African slave.

The obeahman's clients, mostly women, reportedly had to have sex with the monkey to have their desires fulfilled. Their wishes ranged from success in a matter before the courts to gaining a much coveted job or promotion to victory over a troublesome enemy. Even high marks on a college exam. On many occasions, Miss Jen had brazenly threatened someone who had crossed her, shouting that she would not hesitate to "go to Mount Rosser and fuck with the monkey again" if they did not stop provoking her. The threat often worked, but Miss Jen's involvement in obeah practices had a profound and lasting impact on Mordechai.

❁

Mrs. Doris Fagan-Brown was one of my best students. Intelligent, meticulous and diligent, she could be depended on to ask stimulating and thought-provoking questions that enlivened the class. The course I was lecturing at the time, Introduction to Theories of Personality, at a rural university in Jamaica, was an intense summer course with some fifty-two students eager to acquire completing credits in Psychology to satisfy graduation requirements. But Mrs. Fagan-Brown was a consistent 'A' student and always turned in excellent work.

A matronly mother of two young children, and just in her late thirties, she was also polite and friendly, always greeting you with a smile. But when an eating disorder she developed led to weight gain, she became very self-conscious, at times feeling intimidated by other women.

Two days after the September 11 terrorist attacks in New York, I was returning marked research assignment papers to the students in the class. I openly congratulated Mrs. Fagan-Brown on her brilliant research paper, which had earned her a well-deserved A+. It was a gesture meant to also encourage her peers. Her classmates shouted and applauded her for the admirable work she had turned in, particularly because of the complexity of her selected research topic, "Is Racism a Mental Disorder?" on which there had been little research previously published.

But that day she looked rather subdued, unsmiling and seemingly emotionless, accepting the praise quietly and humbly, then mumbling brief thanks before taking her seat at the rear of the classroom. Later on, after dismissal, she approached me and asked if she could have a brief word with me. I was rushing out to another class, so I told her to meet me at my faculty office around noon.

She was already waiting when I arrived at the reception area, so I invited her in, waited until she had settled into one of the chairs facing the desk, and apologized for not being able to attend to her before.

"Oh, that's quite alright, Prof. My next class is at three o'clock this afternoon, so it was no problem waiting for you. Please forgive me, but I would like to consult you on a certain matter. It's something personal. I know that you are busy, but I understand that you do private consultations."

"Yes, I do, but not on campus. I do sessions by appointment at the Pastoral Centre most evenings and on weekends if necessary. When could you come in?" I asked.

"Any day this week. Whenever you say. But it's not really for me, Prof. It is my husband who needs your assistance. I have been trying for quite a while now to convince him to seek professional help, and he has finally agreed to do so. I told him about you and he says he's willing to see you."

"Very good. We could meet on Thursday afternoon at four. Would that be alright for him?" I asked.

"Certainly, sir. I will be accompanying him, so I will ensure that we're there on time. I thank you so much; I am sure you can help him. He has been so reluctant to seek counselling, but I think he now realizes that he needs it urgently," she replied, fidgeting nervously with an umbrella on her lap.

"Doris, tell me about your husband and what the problem seems to be, as far as you know," I said while reaching for a notepad nearby.

"Doctor, my husband is having serious problems, and I am afraid that he could be suicidal. What I mean is that he has been acting strange, taking unnecessary, dangerous risks with his life, like when driving alone. Folks have seen him on the road and they tell me. He is not sleeping, and he spends a lot of time by himself in his study. Plus a whole lot of other things. I don't know if I can describe everything...I..." she muttered.

"It's okay, Doris, take your time. Tell me, how old is he? What kind of work does he do? And how long have you been married?"

"He's thirty four; two years younger than I am. We have been married for six years now, and we have two lovely boys. My husband is a pastor, a reverend in the church, and he counsels and has helped a lot of people as part of his ministerial duties, but he doesn't seem to be able to help himself or solve his own personal problems," she explained.

"What do you know about those personal problems he is having? Has he discussed them with you, or did you just happen to find out? Give me your perspective on the whole situation."

"It is a very complex one, and it is affecting the children, it is affecting me, and, of course, it is having a serious effect on our relationship too. Although he is a pastor he doesn't believe in God; he is an atheist. He has told me on many occasions that the story about Jesus, Heaven and Hell and the second coming is pure foolishness. According to him, it is a deception to control the minds of people and maintain the establishment and keep the ruling class in positions of power," Doris revealed. "It is really hard to understand what's going on in his mind. He is a very good preacher, very dynamic and persuasive, but he says that when he goes to preach on Sundays he is just doing a job; he goes to work, just like any other paid employment because he's got to survive and has a family to take care of. He says he doesn't believe that there is a God. He says that there is just not enough evidence to show that God really exists."

Added Doris: "The other thing that really worries me a lot is that he is spending a lot of time by himself locked up in his study, sometimes up to three o'clock in the morning, before he comes to bed...I don't..." she said, before trailing off. She was on the verge of tears.

"But being a pastor with many responsibilities, wouldn't he be in there preparing his sermons or maybe dealing with other church matters or problems? I asked, taking advantage of her moment of silence.

"He never prepares his sermons beforehand; like he doesn't need to, he is very good at improvising and would just as quickly select a passage out of the Bible, and while on his feet at the pulpit facing a fairly large congregation, deliver an inspiring and impressive sermon for which he is usually warmly thanked and congratulated. On several occasions, while driving to church, he would ask me to read aloud a certain Bible passage. Then, for the next ten minutes or so, he would construct an outline of the sermon in his mind," said Doris. "I know that he is using drugs; he secretly smokes ganja[8]. He never does it in front of me, but

I know. And he spends a lot of time looking at pornography on the computer. When I found out and asked him about it, he said he was doing important research. He claims it is necessary for his ministerial and Christian counselling duties."

"Mrs. Brown, tell me, what is your relationship like? I mean the intimacy and the whole dynamics of your marriage, communication, commitment and so on. Also, what about faithfulness and jealousy? Is that an issue?" I asked.

"Yes, it is a big problem. I don't know if he still loves me. We have not been intimate for quite a while; it's like he has lost interest in me or maybe I am no longer attractive to him. I don't really think there is anything wrong with him sexually because he is so hooked to those blue movies, and he also masturbates pretty often. I see evidence of it all the time, but I don't say anything to him about it."

"Do you know if there is some other woman involved, or anyone else for that matter? I asked, watching her mannerisms for hidden emotions.

"To be honest, I can't say for sure, but it is possible. Of course, there is gossip among the folks at church about him and some of the young church sisters, but nothing really concrete or substantial. If there was anything concrete, I would have heard. The busybodies and gossipmongers in the congregation would make sure that I know about it."

"When did all this become obvious to you? Because surely, things must have been somewhat good or normal earlier on, like when you just got married or sometime after."

"Oh yes. Things were more or less okay with us until about two years ago. We were fairly happy then, just like any normal couple I suppose. I knew that he didn't grow up in a wholesome environment with his mother and siblings, but I was so in love with him that I sort of turned a blind eye to all that. Maybe I was hoping that he would settle down to a good family life and live up to his obligations of setting a standard and an example for others as a pastor, as a man of God. But as we say here in Jamaica, the man just change like a green lizard. It is really unbelievable."

❂

Samantha Wallace was worried. Anyone could tell by her state of anxiety and confusion. It was not like her. A dynamic sales supervisor with a large commodities distributor, she had been taking a number of subjects in the Behavioural Sciences, seeking a Bachelors degree in Human Resource Administration. She had requested a meeting with me to discuss her elderly father, who she said was 'behaving like a mad man', what with taking up with a girl who could be his granddaughter, bringing shame and disgrace upon his family.

"Doc, the thing is that my father is almost eighty years old. He will be eighty in December, his grandchildren are in their thirties and he has two great-grands. It is really terrible that he is seeing this young girl. I understand that she is nineteen or twenty. I mean, how can that be? She is just exploiting him for real," said Samantha.

Her concern was understandable. As the youngest of his daughters, she was very close to him. She lived fairly close to his home and saw to his well-being. So she had quickly become aware that her dad was often having a sleepover female visitor, and later on she found out that it was the young girl.

Samantha's father had been widowed just three years before, following the death of her bedridden mother, who had succumbed to lung cancer. The old man, however, was in remarkably good health due to a vigorous and active physical lifestyle as a farmer, and was known to still have a sweet tooth for the younger females in the semi-rural district where he owned large tracts of fertile land.

"Samantha, do you think this could be a serious relationship that your dad is in with this girl or just a temporary fling that will soon fizzle out?" I asked.

"I am the one who handles everything for him, anything to do with his business or finances. I sign on his accounts, pay his bills, buy groceries and see to it that he goes for regular medical check-ups and so on. I also give him some pocket money every week," she said. "First thing I noticed is that he started asking me for more money on his allowance, at times double or triple what I used to withdraw for him. And it is just since he started fooling around with this…this brazen hussy. She's just after his money, that's all. I know that he gives her money all the time. She has a small daughter and no father for the child, at least none we see anywhere around. Please, sir, I would like you to talk to him, to counsel him. He needs it."

"Well, Samantha, have you discussed the whole matter with him, and have you suggested that he come in for counselling? Does he agree with you that there are problems regarding his liaison with such a young lady?" I asked.

"No, Doc, I really have not asked him anything about it. On that occasion when I saw her at the house, I just asked him who she was, and he said that she comes in twice a week to do some house-cleaning and look after his clothes. I know that that is not true because there is someone, an older lady, who does that every Saturday. I did not want to argue with him over that, so I just left it there," Samantha said. "What I could tell him is that you want to see him to talk to him. I am sure that he will agree. As a matter of fact, he does have some degree of memory loss, and at times he is absent-minded. It is not yet very serious, but I could refer to that problem as the reason for a consultation with you. At least he is aware of that difficulty he's been having, and he speaks about it too."

"Okay, Samantha, I tell you what. Call me at the Pastoral Centre on Tuesday afternoon to confirm an appointment with your father for Wednesday morning at ten. I will do an assessment of the situation with him, then we'll determine the best approach to take. I will do whatever I can to help."

❁

The first thing that struck me about Mordechai and Doris Brown was the major physical difference between them. Doris was the typical motherly housewife committed to home and family. She was short with a cute face and an engaging smile. Appearing a bit subdued and introspective initially, Pastor Mordechai Brown was handsome with a well-proportioned physique. The voluptuousness of his lips and his large, pensive eyes added to the undeniable magnetic attractiveness that made him a popular preacher, who was greatly admired by his congregation, particularly the young women.

But at the time of our meeting, Mordechai was on the verge of being defrocked and removed from the church ministry, as senior church members had became aware of some of his scandalous escapades with a number of young women in the church. All this was fairly well known to most folks in the church, yet his wife was reluctant to tell me about it, perhaps out of embarrassment or determination to protect her husband and family. After going through some preliminaries with them, I asked Doris to leave us alone for a while. She was reluctant at first, but after brief hesitation, she went out to the reception area, where she sat quietly for about forty-five minutes.

Being an experienced Christian counsellor, Pastor Brown was aware of the importance of candid disclosure in a therapeutic session, so he quite willingly shared with me his most intimate thoughts, his unique personal experiences, his hopes and fears, and the intense emotions that often moved him to engage in risky behaviour.

"Doctor, as you can well imagine, I have tried in every way possible and with all the knowledge and experience I have acquired through many years in the ministry to deal with these personal problems that are plaguing me, but to no avail. They seem to be getting worse. I mean unmanageable," he said. "And the irony of it all is that so often I've helped many individuals and families overcome serious crises in their lives. I have genuinely helped many, not only my own church members, but many others in the parish through our long-standing community outreach and assistance programs, yet I am unable to help myself. It makes me feel so inadequate," he explained in an easy and casual manner, seeming relieved at the opportunity to discharge some of the psycho-emotional burden he had been struggling with.

"Pastor, how long has it been since these problems began? And did anything significant or stressful happen around that same time?" I asked.

"Well, things started to deteriorate some three years ago. I really don't remember anything special or stressful happening then, apart from my elevation to full ministry when I was assigned a circuit of four churches in the district. But that was something good for my career and my personal development. It was something I was looking forward to," he explained.

"Well, as you know, Pastor, there are events in our lives that we classify as good or desirable, things we yearn for and eagerly want to happen, like winning the lottery, getting married, receiving a job promotion or welcoming a new born child, and so on. But in truth and in fact, our inner reaction to them is roughly equivalent to the emotional and physiological turbulence we undergo when we react to some other shocking or distressing experience," I told him. "Often they qualify as real stressors for us, since their effect, though not obvious for the single event itself, do accumulate along with other minor hassles to build up into almost permanent or chronic states of anxiety and depression, which can lead to dysfunctional behaviour generally. Then, of course, there is always the potential danger of suicide, especially in the presence of major depressive disorder," I explained while he listened attentively.

I then instructed him to paint a picture of the two main aspects of his life: his family life at home and his church ministry.

"At home, the children are really a source of joy and pride for us both. No problem there, but when it comes to the intimate side of our married life, that's another story. It seems that I have lost interest in Doris; the sexual thing. I don't know, but I just

don't feel for it at all. I mean, we get along quite well otherwise. We talk and communicate on almost any subject, and I
love her very much," he said. "It's just that the kind of love I
have for her seems to have changed. I see her more as a sister,
an aunt, or some friend or relative, even as a mother. She is a
very good mother to the children, and she has great qualities.
It's just that the passion and physical attraction I had for her is
definitely not there anymore. It's like the chemistry is gone."

Pastor Brown's words came across in a monotone, as if he
was distracted by other things. It was the first time that he was
telling someone that he was married to a woman he no longer
loved in a passionate and sexual way. His attitude towards her
was a patronizing one, and he spoke down to her with an almost
snobbish and arrogant haughtiness.

"Now, tell me, Pastor, has there been anyone else, some
other significant person who has come into your life, maybe
someone who is emotionally or sentimentally important to
you?" I asked.

He looked at me with a slightly surprised look, and then
tightened his lips together in a vain attempt to suppress a revealing smile. It was obvious that I had touched on a sensitive issue,
but by this time there was not much resistance on his part since
an understanding based on trust and mutual respect had been
established between us.

"Well, to be honest, I do think there is someone like that,
but I have made all efforts not to allow that situation to interfere
with my family life or with my work in the church," he said.

Although Mordechai Brown tried to downplay what turned
out to be a torrid extra-marital affair he was having with a young

member of his congregation, it turned out that this relationship was the cause of most of his recent psycho-emotional distress and associated problems. There had been other minor flings he had immersed himself in with the reckless gusto of a drunken sailor.

It was, however, an entirely different situation with Nekeisha, who had recently left Kingston for rural Manchester and had brought with her the full repertoire of street-smart tricks and cunning devices she had used to survive in the tough slums of Kingston. From the first moment he saw her on that Sunday in church, he felt a sexual desire for her. He vividly remembered how she sat innocently on one of the front pews, and how he did not in the least suspect that this waif-thin, seventeen-year-old girl would soon exert a magnetic pull and troublesome influence upon him.

Shortly after her arrival they started seeing each other privately, under the guise of providing her with some counselling and spiritual advice. But these meetings quickly turned into regular intimate sessions during which they indulged in prolonged bouts of unbridled sex, exploring a variety of truly bizarre activities that most folks would describe as downright sick and abnormal. It was an unholy coming together of two hungry souls that rapidly evolved into a fornicatory circus of forbidden pleasures.

Growing up in the harsh inner-city slums of Kingston, Nekeisha had been initiated into the ghetto's subculture of drugs, sex and pervasive violence and criminality from an early age. Her parents had sent her off to the district of Heartease in Manchester to stay with relatives, hoping that under their wholesome influence she'd be reformed.

Mordechai went on to vividly describe the sinking feeling he experienced on the day he realized that he had lost his career in the church ministry. It happened in the middle of an emergency meeting of the church board to which he had been summoned. There he was, trying to convince the board and his bishop that the eager gossipmongers in his congregation were simply determined to get rid of him. But the bishop had replied, "My son, please. I beg of you, do not add hypocrisy to the abundance of your other sins."

Mordechai felt he had been called to the meeting so that this insulting slap to his face could be applied right before church board officials. Two days after the uncomfortable board meeting, he got a letter informing him that he was being temporarily suspended from the church ministry. It was only then that he decided to come in for counselling.

"Are you still seeing that young lady, Pastor?" I asked.

"Unfortunately, yes, though we don't see each other as often as before. I am earnestly making all efforts to break off the connection, but I find it extremely difficult to do so. Seeing her and spending even two hours or so with her seems to be the only way I can achieve some kind of relief from all the tension and the anxiety I've been going through. I just cannot resist her, and it really has me baffled," he explained.

"So, when was the last time? I would like you to describe that encounter, but also tell me what was happening immediately before you made the decision to meet with her on that particular occasion," I said.

"Well, the last time we met was around two weeks ago. One of my brothers has this girlfriend, a nurse, who is aware of the situation, and is someone we can trust. We've been meeting at her apartment. The thing is, I vowed that it would not happen again. Several times I've sworn, taken an oath that it's finished!

And I'm able to hold on to that for a few days, but soon after I find myself calling her," he explained.

"Does this sense of powerlessness also extend to other aspects of you life, Pastor? Do you find it difficult to stick to a decision or resolution you've made in other matters?" I asked.

"Oh no, Doc, I am quite firm and consistent when it comes to holding to a decision. I don't think I have a problem there. That is why I find my submissiveness to Nekeisha's every little fancy kind of weird, really strange, because it's not like me. I am accustomed to being in control, to always lead out, at all times," he replied.

"So what accounts for the terrific hold this girl has over you, Pastor? We'll have to determine exactly what it is so that we can focus our analysis and therapeutic efforts in that direction. Does she remind you of someone or something perhaps, maybe related to some past experience?"

"Doc, I *do* know what it is. It's nothing more than the sex. Yes, that's really what it is. I have absolutely no doubts about that. As a matter of fact, were it not for that, I'm pretty sure I could handle the situation easily." This, he offered with such assertiveness that it caused me to immediately suspect his dilemma to be an overwhelming obsessive-compulsive engrossment of his sexual faculties.

"Sure, I understand. I would like you to share with me the details of your intimate encounters with Nekeisha. But first, we'll do a little relaxation exercise, okay? Very simple and easy. It's quite pleasant and..." I was speaking in the warmest and most inviting manner possible, when I was cut short by his sudden interjection.

"Please, no hypnosis, Doc! I don't want to be hypnotized. I...I don't believe in it, and really, I would rather not, okay?" he pleaded.

"It's alright, Pastor. I just want you to sort of tune in to every cell in your body, fully activate and energize them so that you may access and use up all the dormant powers you have there. It's really a basic and well-known technique. We have a fancy name for the procedure; it's called systematic desensitization, but it's really rather simple. Okay, just lie back comfortably... right. Uncross your legs...good. Close your eyes...now take deep rhythmic breaths...inhale, then slowly out...again, yes, slowly out...good...and relax, yes, relax.

"Now I want you to focus entirely on your toes..., yes, put your mind down there..., concentrate and try to feel the insides of your toes without moving them, starting with the little toes, then slowly go across to the big toe. Feel the bones and joints deep inside, feel the blood circulating in them. Then relax them. Let them go to sleep, quietly... softly.

"Now slowly go to the soles of your feet, and then to your ankles...now gradually come up your legs...your knees. Feel the energy coursing deep within them ...slow...now your hips right around...come up slowly into your belly...your organs, feel the insides of them...yes, now easy up into your chest, feel your heart pumping...the blood force surging through...go right around your back, up to your shoulders...now down your arms, elbows...slowly down to your wrists, your hands, fingers...feel your fingernails at the tips...let them relax, easily...good.

"Now slowly reverse from your fingertips and up your wrists...your hands, up both forearms to your elbows, arms, shoulders...and up your neck...feel the pulsating blood going up into your head. You are inside your mouth now. Feel your tongue, teeth; now you easily float into your head…go right into the middle…just behind your eyes…good. You are now in the centre of your brain, within the limbic system…seated on your psychic throne, the little pineal gland…your command centre. You are your very own master there and whatever you will, all powers of doing are yours, fully, totally yours. Feel and taste the irresistible power that is yours…from head to toes…entirely you…now breathe…breathe and relax…"

I had easily guided Mordechai Brown into a pre-hypnotic trance, a moderately deep state of mind-body relaxation. I quietly moved away from his side, retrieved my writing pad and guided him into a smooth narrative involving the steamy, sexual proclivities of his erotic young temptress, Nekeisha.

❂

Samantha Wallace accompanied her father to our scheduled therapeutic session, and after a brief introduction, I assured her that it was okay for her to leave him and return within an hour or so for him since she had a few urgent matters to attend to in the town centre.

Mr. Leopold Newton turned out to be a very jovial and pleasant older gentleman. He had a contagious sense of humour and an energetic disposition that would easily win him friends. I immediately noticed that his handshake was firm and his voice vigorous and deep. His whole body movements and demeanour indicated high levels of energy. For his age, he sparkled with exuberance.

"Mr. Newton, welcome, sir. It's a pleasure meeting you. How are you doing today?" I asked.

"Oh, very well. Thank the Lord that so far I'm in fairly good health. Just had a check-up sometime last week, and they said that I am as strong as an ox. Well, I was never a sickly person at all. The only thing is that at times I forget little things here and there, like where I put down a tool, or even at times I forget where I've tied up a goat or so. But I have a few young guys who help me around so I don't complain," he explained while consistently maintaining good eye contact.

"I'm sure you are happy to have such a caring daughter. Samantha is one of my best students, a hard worker too. Please, do have a seat… good," I said.

"Thank you. Yes, she's the last one, and the most dependable and helpful of all my children. But she worries too much about me; sometimes even wants to treat me as if I am one of her sons instead of her father. But I don't mind it at all, for she's really a good daughter to me," he continued in a voice made raspy by age.

"Alright, Sir Leopold, I just need a little background information on you; basic stuff, nothing too complicated. Then I'll go on to check your memory function, and if necessary I'll recommend something for any problems there. I'll also show you a few memory tricks you could try. They're called mnemonics, and they are quite easy. They should help you keep track of those little things you tend to forget," I said. "You said that Samantha worries too much about you. What exactly is she worried about, knowing that, even at your age, you are in fairly good health?" I asked.

"My daughter is too concerned about the people in the district and what they say. My wife, that's her mother, died over two years ago, and I mean, I'm still strong and healthy. I eat good food, work hard everyday in my field, I drink my roots wine regularly, and I boil my herbs and roots tonic myself. So just because I talk to the girls in the district…you know what I mean. I am a friendly guy, Doc, and to be honest, the older women really don't turn me on. It's the truth."

Sir Leopold, as he was called, was speaking in a very relaxed manner, giving an almost casual, unhurried picture of how he was living out and thoroughly enjoying his golden years.

"Perhaps she's concerned that these girls could take advantage of you, exploit you and take your money and all that. Or maybe even get you into some kind of trouble?" I noted.

"My daughter just doesn't know. Maybe that's what she thinks, but the girlfriend I have now is only eighteen. She already has a baby, but she's the one that keeps me feeling young and strong. I have no complaints about her, but I am not fooling myself that she's going to stay with me forever. I am almost eighty so I am enjoying it while it lasts. We are good for each other, so what the hell. Do you blame me, Doc?" he asked with a broad smile and twinkling, mischievous eyes.

"Surely not, Sir Leopold, surely not. I think your attitude to that important aspect of your life is a healthy one, as long as you remain sober and wide-eyed about this girl. On the other hand, let's be realistic about it, eh? You wouldn't want her to become pregnant, right? And then again, are you contemplating marrying her or somehow settling down to a permanent arrangement with her?"

"Of course not. It's just that my daughter Samantha, being the youngest of my children, is not aware of the wily old fox that her dad is. The truth is that none of these young girls can put one over on me. No, not at all. At least not so easily. You know what I mean; when they are going, I've already gone and come back," he boasted. "The young lady's name is Tatiana; she's smart and we've reasoned quite frankly and openly about our relationship. We both know what we want out of it: no dishonesty at all. We talk and understand each other very well. So, for now we are happy with each other. But we try to keep everything very discreet and quiet. The district is small and the people around don't mind their own business, but I don't have a problem at all, Doc."

Meanwhile, I was carrying out a careful but subtle assessment of Mr. Newton, a holistic mind-body appreciation of his persona. He had, over his long years, evidently forged a philosophy of life and a set of practical coping skills that secured him a generally healthy and vigorous old age. And even more important was the fact that he had developed a certain toughness, an uncommon synchronization of physical, mental and spiritual capacities that allows an individual to face challenges smoothly and with total confidence.

It was obvious that his daughter was hoping that I would somehow persuade the old man to change his hedonistic ways, maybe even break off his liaison with young Tatiana and take up with a mature and respectable lady she would approve of. My better judgement told me that not only would this be a futile effort, but that if Sir Leopold attempted to veer from the life he knew at this stage of his journey, the very holistic harmony that had served him so well throughout the years would become fragmented and he would be thrown into a state of imbalance, unhappiness and ill health.

It has been seven years since I had three therapy sessions with Mr. Newton. Over the years he kept in touch with us, occasionally stopping by and bringing us a lot of produce from his farmlands. Each time he visited, he looked just as hearty and strong as ever. On one occasion he announced that Tatiana, who had become his common-law wife,[9] had given birth to a bouncing baby girl. Samantha was no longer Sir Leopold's youngest child.

✹

Pastor Mordechai Brown said he fell for Nekeisha's free-spirited nature.

"What I find so attractive and fascinating about Nekeisha is that she is totally without shame, there's really no pretence at all with her; she is just natural and carefree. The times we've been together, well, it's like I am in a kind of limbo, totally absorbed in her and her cute little antics," he explained. "Some two months ago, when I managed to arrange things so that we could spend three full days together, she fully revealed herself to me. It was unbelievable and a bit frightening for me the things she would do. I wasn't expecting that she would be so skilful and so experienced and..., " he said before pausing, as the blended images of skin, flesh and erotic shapes flashed across the screen of his mind.

"Please continue. Things like what?" I softly encouraged.

"Well, first she was begging me to hurt her, to spank and beat her. This was actually before we started making love. Of course, I refused, but after realizing that this was like a habit with her, I beat her with a belt on her bottom so that she could get turned on. She was really enjoying it and demanded that I do it harder and harder. She's a sadist for sure. Right, Doc?"

"Well, no, Pastor, she's not. In this case she's a masochist, that is, the one who experiences sexual pleasure by receiving pain, by being controlled and humiliated as part of the erotic love play. In fact, you would more be the one with sadistic inclinations, that is, the one who inflicts the pain and other acts of sexual cruelty on the one he loves and deriving sexual pleasure from it," I explained.

At the time, I was seated out of his visual range, actually behind him, as he relaxed in a comfortably recumbent position on the large leather couch. Pastor Brown went on to describe the tattooed butterfly on Nekeisha's back, right between her shoulders, the tattooed rose on her pubic mound, and several discreetly hidden body piercings. She had small rings on her navel and on her plump vulva. But he had the greatest fascination with the removable tongue-stud[10] she wore whenever they met away from the church environs.

He graphically described the sexualized chaos they forged under the aphrodisiac effects of the sinsemilla, a potent variety of Jamaican marijuana. As she moaned, he would enter her without a care in the world. While relating the intensely erotic experience, Pastor Brown was also reliving the torrid events through vivid flashbacks on the screen of his mind.

"You have recognized that your liaison with the young lady is one that is fraught with disastrous possibilities, Pastor. And as you stated before, it's really a fast road to damnation and total catastrophe for you and your family," I remarked.

"I have decided to end it permanently. It has been like a nightmare from the first day that girl came into the church. If I didn't know better I would think that she was some kind of sexual demon or a fallen angel that was sent directly to destroy me. Just a few days ago I was turning it over in my mind. I said to myself that all this didn't happen just by chance. Nekeisha came into my life like a maddening angel of lust with the sole purpose of robbing me of my sanity," he replied.

"Pastor, you are a man of faith and prayer, and as they say, one who is anointed of the Lord. Are you implying that this teenager has managed to obliterate all that, to drag you down from your tower of strength, from all the fortitude and sound judgment that your training and many years in the ministry have instilled in you?" I asked.

"Well, Doc, it would seem so, but my ideas about all that are somewhat different from the average folk out there and very dissimilar from the comforting beliefs held by many of my fellow pastors and theologians," he replied. "You see, I pray for others, but not for me. In fact, I never pray for myself. I encourage strong faith in my flock and in all others as a means of instilling hope and optimism into those who are devastated and suffering the vicissitudes of life. But, Doc, it's only as a means of providing some comfort for them, like therapy, very similar to what you do here with your psychological techniques and treatment," he further revealed.

He added: "Although I do have a serious responsibility as the pastor and spiritual guide of the church, there are many things that I do not share with them, things that I never discuss with the ordinary believer. And it would be stupid of me to do so. I do not believe that there is a God at all; there is just not enough evidence to warrant such a conclusion. The whole idea just does not fit with a calmly reasoned and realistic view of life.

It's all based on mere assumptions, Doc. Of course, I recognize that the concept of God is necessary for an understanding of life for most folk out there," he continued, pausing for a moment to gather and organize his thoughts. I seized the opportunity to put another question to him.

"Do you experience any difficulties in reconciling your personal ideas about the existence of God with your preaching to others that they must believe in the same God you don't think exists at all? How do you reconcile these opposite poles within yourself, Pastor?" I asked matter-of-factly.

"At times I do feel uncomfortable about it, Doc, but only in the sense that I know the truth, yet I am not only concealing the truth from them, but in effect fooling them, leading them down a rosy path based on the imaginings of some clever fellows of old, and this book, the Bible, that many regard as some kind of a magical book," he answered. "I think they are victims of organized religion, of men of power playing upon people's psychology of fear to influence and frighten them, to distort their views and to poison their reasoning. It is all so brazenly intolerant and absurd. To be honest, the reason I am still in the church is because of necessity, but it is getting to me. I mean it is a tough, dishonourable way to make a living, like some kind of a con man peddling the proverbial snake oil cure-all to gullible people. Really, it is very hard, because I am living a constant lie. I've got to be ready with the right Bible quote to support my persuasive lies and deceptions…. It is..," he said before losing track of his train of thought.

"Can you remember exactly when you started having these ideas, or when you arrived at those conclusions?" I quietly prompted, taking advantage of the lingering silence enveloping our exchange.

"I think I began having serious doubts about God and religion when I started keeping the Seventh Day Sabbath on Saturdays. On Sundays, I worked myself up to a frenzy of religious ecstasy to deliver a convincing sermon, careful not to reveal anything about my private observance of the so-called Sabbath to the members," Pastor Brown revealed. "I would be in serious trouble with the bishop and church officials if they knew about it. It was sometime after that it dawned on me that I was engaging in some serious deception, hypocrisy, real unadulterated duplicity. So it started getting harder and harder for me to stand there facing those nice, simple folk just to manipulate their beliefs and give them a good feeling, knowing that it's all a lie. Most of them would be really shocked to know that their preacher is an atheist, a liar and a deceiver. Don't you agree, Doc?"

"Yes, I certainly agree. They would be freaked out, psyched out of their minds, as they say out there. But I don't think you are a true atheist in the generally accepted sense of the word. I would say instead that you are more of an agnostic. Don't you accept that there is some kind of superior intelligence, some master creative power that brought everything into existence, even if it's not a God as such?" I asked.

"Oh yes, absolutely, but it's all pure energy residing in everything that exists in nature, water, heat, the very soil and stones. Not that utterly indifferent God outside of us that men have created in their imagination. I am sure that this may sound weird, but I am convinced that we, all of us, are our own personal God, and when we pray, it is really to ourselves that we pray.

We are on a spiritual journey towards becoming that perfect, omniscient and omnipotent being we yearn for. That's what I know, but it is not something I care to discuss with the average person out there," he shared. "Then, of course, when Nekeisha came along, all my learning and experience were of no use to me. It was like I had no will power at all. For me, she became like a she-demon in the church, a succubus[11] of unbridled lust that was sent directly to get me. It got so bad for me that I had to ask her not to sit at the front in church. I usually had to avoid looking in her direction so as to avoid being distracted and getting an erection right there at the pulpit, which would be embarrassing to say the least, eh?"

"Oh, most certainly it would. But please continue, Pastor," I politely urged him on.

"Well, it was my involvement with this girl that got me into using drugs regularly, mainly marijuana, and getting into extreme pornography, which she was addicted to. And then, instead of trying to rescue her from all those malevolent activities, I joined her. My wife had been at me to seek professional help because she saw the danger signs all around, but I was too enmeshed into all that self-destructive lifestyle with this youngster. It was only after I started having some weird masturbatory fantasies that I realized I had to stop and do something about it," the pastor explained.

"Please describe those fantasies. What were they exactly, and when did they take place. I mean, under what circumstances? I asked.

"Well, I found that I could not make love to my wife in the usual way; I had to put certain pictures in my mind so as to get an erection and be able to function with her. I had to close my eyes and imagine one of my sisters-in-law or one of my wife's friends. On other occasions I would try to picture Nekeisha, but strange enough I just couldn't bring her face or anything else about her into my imagination. There was a blockage in my mind preventing me from visualizing her, but I could easily bring the picture of my sister-in-law to mind and achieve quick ejaculation. Afterwards I would feel very bad about the whole thing and would be miserable for the next few hours until eventually it wore off. Of course, I didn't tell Doris anything about it, but that is what eventually persuaded me to come to see you."

In my notepad I jotted down the term Situational E.D. (erectile dysfunction/ impotence), which refers to the failure of a man to achieve a satisfactory erection with his regular partner or with certain partners, or in certain circumstances or places. It is an intrapsychic[12] condition that operates mainly at the subconscious level and physically plays out as the inability to achieve or maintain a strong erection.

The therapeutic approach we adopted with Pastor Brown involved classical modes of depth psychology and techniques of cognitive behavioural therapy (CBT). The objective was to, first of all, probe the unconscious for repressed, disturbing mental entities which he needs to confront and come to terms with. The cognitive and behavioural techniques would help him to modify his patterns of response to tempting stimuli and strengthen his resolve and will power. He continued in the psychological counselling program for some five months, at the end of which he had gained considerable functional mastery over his personal, family and professional lives.

Of course, we rarely escape the consequences of our choices and our actions, and so it was with Pastor Mordechai Brown. He was eventually defrocked and removed from the ministry; thrown off the pulpit by his tough and unforgiving church superiors. They did not even consider a transfer to some other remote diocese. This development meant a new and troubling source of stress for him and his family.

After he discussed the matter with me, I called on a good friend of mine whom I had not seen for over two years, the Reverend Ransford Maddix, who was at the time a senior chaplain with Jamaica's Correctional Services. Maddix, a sensitive and compassionate cleric, fully understood the plight Pastor Brown faced and promised to assist him in any way he could. A few weeks later we got the good news that Mordechai Brown had been appointed an assistant chaplain with responsibilities for ministering to inmates at several prisons in the correctional system.

He successfully settled into this new position, and his wife Doris also did exceptionally well in the course she was pursuing at college, earning several distinctions and placing first in her class. They both continued to keep in touch with me for a while until I left the area to pursue new challenges.

❁

CHAPTER FOUR

Like a Cup of Trembling

"...for in their youth they lay with her, and they bruised the breasts of her virginity, and poured their whoredoms upon her."

Ezekiel 23: 8-9

One afternoon while running errands: shopping, mailing stuff, getting a prescription filled for an ailing colleague, and so on, my mind kept going back to a mysterious term paper with an incorrect cover page I came across earlier in the day while marking some papers. The student, Carla Kamron, was a quiet, fairly good looking but shy and withdrawn young lady who always sat at the far left corner at the back of the classroom and never participated in class discussions. She didn't seem to have any friends among the students at the college.

In a country with a majority of its people being blacks of African descent, she was in the minuscule minority of light-skinned individuals, or almost-white 'brownings', as they are called. But in the mid-island parish of Saint Elizabeth where she hails from, there are areas where a substantial number of these folks reside. They are said to be descendants of sailors of a nineteenth century German shipwreck who wound up on a treacherous strip of Jamaica's windy south coast before eventually settling in the nearby hills, forming small townships and never returning to Europe. Carla was around twenty-three years old, but because she was short, petite and slim, she looked much younger.

The next day in class, before actually embarking on the subject matter, I began returning the graded papers with the usual congratulatory remarks for the top three. I left Carla's paper for the last, and when she approached my desk with an outstretched hand expecting to receive her folder, I quietly said to her, "Miss Kamron, I need to speak to you about this term paper. Please see me at the faculty office during the noon break, okay?"

"Oh, why, is something wrong with it, Prof?" she replied, looking rather frightened then perplexed.

"It's alright, Carla, don't worry. There's just something here that I need to talk to you about. So just come to the office at that time. Do relax and take it easy." I tried to calm and reassure her due to the worried look and nervous mannerisms she displayed. I kept the folder with me, and she quietly returned to her seat.

Because I taught three classes in the morning session on Tuesdays and had the afternoon free, I allowed students to consult with me on academic matters in the afternoon, though I insist on them setting appointments beforehand. Otherwise, I would be swamped as experience had taught me. When I got to the reception area facing my campus office, I saw four students waiting to see me. One of them, Andrea Newhart, had set an appointment two days before, so I told Carla to wait and that I would see her immediately after.

"Andrea, you said that you wanted to know about making arrangement for some private counselling? As you know, I only deal with academic matters here on campus. But, tell me, what seems to be the problem?" I asked after she had settled into a chair next to my desk.

"Well, Doc, I know that I can talk to you confidentially, and as you have explained on more than one occasion, there must be a relationship of total trust with one's therapist or counsellor for the process to be effective and helpful," said Andrea, a pleasant and attractive young lady with a penetrating intellect and a sharp mind. "There is a serious problem I am having now, well, for the past year and a half. It is really coming from very long ago, but I wasn't aware that anything was wrong. But now it has been acting up on me and affecting me very much," she added, speaking in a low voice, although we were within the privacy of a fairly sound-insulated office.

"Yes, I understand. What I would like you to do is give me a brief outline of the situation as you know it, and then we'll decide how best to proceed from there," I said.

"It's not easy for me to explain. It has to do with my mother, and certain things that happened to me when I was much younger. It's just that I can't understand how she allowed those things to happen, and I am sure she must have known…, and…, and…, oh God. I'm sorry. Maybe I shouldn't say anything about it because she's my mother and I love her," Andrea said as tears welled up in her eyes. She quietly began sobbing. I pulled out a tissue and gave it to her. I didn't say anything for a while to allow the emotional paroxysm to subside a bit.

"It's alright, take it easy now. It is okay to cry. Tears are the mysterious fluid that helps to calm the pains of life and living. Andrea, every problem in life, every situation, has a solution, and very often more than one solution. I will try to help you. Which days would you be available for, say, ninety minute sessions at the Pastoral Centre?" I asked.

After regaining her composure, she gave me a lovely smile, and after agreeing to a time later in the week, she left for her next class. I then asked the receptionist to send in Carla Kamron.

As Carla walked in, I could not help but notice how timid and nervous she looked. She sat at the very edge of the chair with her books and folder in her lap, as if ready to instantly get up and flee. "Carla, please just relax, there is nothing to be apprehensive about. Whatever it is, it's not the end of the world," I assured her.

"But, Prof, all the other students got back their graded papers, and I…, I am the only one that…, well, mine is the only one that was held back, so I don't know," she barely whispered without making eye contact, demurely casting her eyes sideways to the bookshelf then to the abstract painting on the wall. I remained silent, determined not to speak until she looked straight at me. And sure enough, the pregnant silence forced her to look up at me, only to shyly avert her eyes again.

"Miss Kamron, do you have any idea why I asked you to see me? Or, what could be the reason why I did not return your term paper along with the others?" I asked.

"No, Prof, not at all. I really tried to do my best with that assignment. Did I get a failing grade?" she asked shakily.

I took a sustained, analytical look at her which again caused her to momentarily look away, but this time she quickly gathered herself and hesitantly restored eye contact. I handed her the folder and keenly observed as she hastily flipped through the pages, a brief smile lighting up her face as she saw the B plus grade at one of the corners. She then glanced at me with a slightly puzzled look, as if silently asking, *'Well, what's wrong with it?'*

"Please look carefully, Carla. Haven't you noticed something strange on your paper?" I asked, by now really curiously piqued that up to that moment she still hadn't noticed the glaring error on the cover page. She started flipping through the pages again when I decided to interrupt her.

"Would you kindly look at the cover page? The very *first* page," I urged rather impatiently, yet amused that she still had not noticed that her folder had the wrong cover page.

"Oh, my God! I can't believe it! Oh no, how could this happen? And I was so careful, especially when I was preparing the final draft. Please Prof, I don't know what to say. I don't know how I made such a mistake. I was also working on another assignment for my literature course. I don't know how I got the cover pages mixed up. I will do anything at all to make up for the error. Please, sir, I am willing to do an extra task or whatever you ask me to do, I...," she gushed, stumbling over her words.

"Well, I presume that you *did* type an accurate cover page for this paper. Most likely that one is now gracing your literature work. That's *another* mistake you'll also have to correct with your literature professor. Now tell me, Carla, what's happening? Obviously your mind was elsewhere when you were setting up the folders. You were seriously distracted, and you continued to be so absent-minded that even long after, you didn't notice what had transpired."

She listened silently, still holding the folder in her hands and biting her lower lip in an apparent effort to hold back tears of frustration.

"Are you struggling with any major problems, maybe personal or family issues that may be troubling you? Or problems with your studies here? I'm here to help in whichever way I can, and you know very well that you can trust me with confidential matters," I said.

She looked up at me, as if hesitantly weighing options on whether to disclose what she's been keeping to herself.

"No, sir, I'm alright, I am not having any serious problems; I don't know, maybe I just got a bit confused or something, but I am willing to make up for it. Please, sir."

"Good. Tell you what, Miss Kamron; I haven't yet transcribed that grade into the master book. Do the necessary correction and present it to me at the next class, okay? And please strive to be more careful and meticulous with your work. So keep a cool head until then, and have a nice day. Here's my card. If you need to consult me, just call for an appointment." She left, happy with the opportunity to amend the error without it affecting her grade.

After she left, I went on to deal with other students waiting in the foyer. Their issues had to do with questions on research assignments and advice on various academic issues facing them. Shortly after, I rushed to my last class for the day.

❂

An hour after arriving home, having done a few brief meditation exercises, eaten, and settled in for a quiet evening of introspection and planning for the tasks and challenges of the next day, the phone rang. I was determined to ignore it, and eventually the ringing ended. Two minutes later, the phone started ringing again, so I answered.

"Yes, good evening," I said pleasantly.

"Good…, good evening, Doc, I'm sorry to bother you at this time, please forgive me but…"

The voice sounded like that of a young and very nervous female, so I instinctively braced myself and went into my receptive mode for troubled clients, all of whom I have allowed to call me at any time for advice on various problems, but more often crises. I've often wondered if it was a wise thing to do, having been awakened from deep sleep to hear a screaming lady threatening to swallow a whole bottle of sleeping pills she has in her hand, or a young lad suffering from sleep terror disorder just coming out of one of his terrifying nightmares.

"Eh, please…, who is it?" I enquired.

"It's me, Carla. Carla Kamron, sir. I am so sorry to bother you, but I think I left one of my notebooks in your office earlier today. I just can't find it and I need it to complete an assignment. I was just wondering if perhaps you saw it anywhere there," she said.

"Oh, Carla. Well, I doubt it very much. I would have seen it; the office is not so large. Most likely you left it somewhere else. Don't you think so?" I replied, my mind darting from one thing to the other.

"Doc, I have searched everywhere, and I just can't find it. Could you *pleeease* look around in your office to see if I forgot it there. *Pleeease,* sir. I am so worried because I have many important notes in it, and I'll be in serious problems if I can't locate it," she pleaded.

"Miss Kamron, all I can do is check to see if you did leave it in the office, but I won't be going back to campus until three o'clock tomorrow afternoon, so it won't be until that time."

"Oh, yes, that would be quite alright. Thank you, sir, and I am really sorry to bother you. I guess I'm just careless or distracted. I don't know," she offered.

"It's alright, Carla. No need to apologize. It could happen to any of us. I will let you know if I find it, okay? But continue your search in the meantime, as I doubt very much that you left it in the office. So have a good night 'till tomorrow then."

○

At exactly three in the afternoon, as scheduled, I began the symposium lecture in Abnormal Psychology at the small, Grecian-style college amphitheatre filled to capacity with both undergrads and a small number of graduate students. As usual, the topic generated considerable interest among the mixed audience of psychology, sociology, and guidance counselling students, most of them studying for credits in Abnormal Psychology as part of their academic courses.

During a fifteen-minute break, several of the younger students scampered out to the adjoining cafeteria for refreshments and snacks, and I took the opportunity to step outside for some fresh air and to make a quick telephone call. I was walking towards a quiet spot near to one of the side entrances, not looking ahead but concentrating on dialling a number on the phone, when instinctively I made a sudden stop, realizing that I was about to collide with someone ahead of me.

"I am so sorry. I wasn't looking. Oh, it's you, Miss Kamron. I didn't know you'd be at the lecture. I guess I didn't see you in the audience. How are you doing?" I asked rather mechanically as I still wanted to make that call before going back inside the lecture room.

"I am alright, Prof. I was in the hall from the beginning. I find the lecture really interesting. To me, the topic is fascinating. Prof, I know that you are a very busy person, and so I feel bad about giving you so many problems, like with the research paper and then the missing notebook. I am really sorry, sir," she said in a genuine and heartfelt tone.

"That's okay, Carla. Don't worry about it. Did you find the notebook? I must admit that I haven't had a chance to look around for it yet."

Although I was still intent on dialling that telephone number, I couldn't help but notice the delayed answer which eventually came with an underlying hesitancy, a kind of subtle insecurity. "No, Prof, not yet, but I'm still looking for it ..., I..., please excuse me, sir, I am going back inside," she replied as she walked to the open side door.

I decided to give up on the phone call, as the fifteen-minute break was rapidly ticking away. Turning towards the entrance, I suddenly glanced sideways just in time to surprise Carla staring in my direction. She quickly averted her eyes, and I pretended not to see her. When I took my place at the podium to resume the lecture, she was there sitting at one of the front seats slightly to my left, intently scribbling in a notebook on her lap.

For a few brief seconds, I had the subtle impression that she just might have been stalking me; the coincidences and chance encounters were now frequent happenings.

○

Fiona McLaren quietly placed an open folder with a completed personal data form on my desk, slightly leaned forward, and while taking up some files, informed me that Andrea Newhart was outside in the reception area.

"May I send her in, sir?" she asked.

"Yes, but let me glance through this first, okay?" I responded as she walked towards the door. A few minutes later, Andrea came in.

"Good morning, Doc. Sorry to be late, but something came up at home; I had to wait for the plumber to arrive and fix a burst pipe. Hope I didn't throw off your schedule too much?" Andrea seemed so happy and full of energy, with that cute dimpled smile of hers, so disarming and candid in its fresh appeal. It's hard to believe that she was here to discuss distressful matters and to seek solace and emotional help to deal with them.

"Oh no, Andrea, not at all. I've made the necessary adjustments to the other clients' appointments. I do appreciate you calling to let us know that you'd be delayed. Please have a seat. How are you today?" I asked.

"Well, to be honest, I am feeling so nervous. I don't know, but I suppose it's because of what I mentioned to you the other day; those things that are bothering me now. I have never discussed these things with anyone before, much less with an analyst. No one really knows, but I have been living with it for all these years," Andrea said.

"Okay, take it easy now and let's try to relax first. You need to be comfortable, and you need to be confident that there are ways to deal with your situation whatever it may be. It's good that you have taken the first step towards finding a solution to the problem. That is, recognizing that you need help."

"You said that you feel nervous. Is that a feeling you get very often, maybe in particular situations? Try to identify those times when you have felt this way. I mean, what was happening then? What makes you feel nervous now?" I asked.

"Well, Doc, first, I have never been to an analyst, a psychologist, or anyone like that, and I am scared that I may be hypnotized and perhaps go on to do or say things that I shouldn't, not being in full control of myself. So just coming here to see you makes me nervous, Doc."

"Ah, well let me allay some of your fears. I do not inflict pain or discomfort on my clients. Neither do I put them in a hypnotic trance without their previous knowledge. My sole objective is to help with their psycho-emotional distress and with issues of coping and living that they may be struggling with. And all of that happens within a context of complete confidentiality, trust and empathy. It is something I have been doing for decades now."

During the next few minutes, I proceeded to guide her through a few simple techniques of mental blanking and thought bubbling which would help to ensure that she entered a relaxed and receptive state of mind closely resembling the *tabula rasa* or mental blank slate of transcendental meditation.

"Andrea, it is important that you try to identify your feelings and your emotions. Familiarize yourself with them in an intimate way, and you'll find that by so doing you will gradually gain mastery over them. Now, I would like you to just explore that sensation of nervousness that comes over you at times. Then, tell me what you find as you do that."

I already knew that she was struggling with disturbing memories and conflicting emotions that were made even more intractable by the fact that she's been enduring their unsettling effects all by herself. She was living day to day with serious unresolved issues that were weighing heavily on her mind and affecting her functional abilities more and more. As her story unfolded, I hardly found any surprises.

The setting at the Pastoral Centre was conducive to the disclosure, examination, and analysis of things intimate, troubling, nagging and upsetting. Care had been taken to ensure that the therapy room was virtually soundproof, almost at the standard of a recording studio, yet with the cosiness and friendly atmosphere of a home study or side alcove.

Soft, reclining lounge chairs, a leather couch, nature paintings, potted plants and barely discernible classical music in the background were all intended to quiet the senses and calm the soul to foster the understanding, trust and confidentiality that are essential for a successful intervention.

"Tell me about your relationship with your parents. You are an only child, right? And you grew up entirely with mom and dad?" I asked as she nodded in agreement to my probing questions.

She slowly began unfolding the tapestry of her life as if she was speaking to a trusted friend. Her father had been good and supportive, though a bit distant due to demands of his job as a technical supervisor at a large industrial chemical plant. He had become morose and gloomy after suffering a serious work-related injury a few years ago that kept him confined to bed most of the time. Andrea was very close to her mother whom she described as a dedicated housewife, pious and committed to the Catholic Church.

Her mother was relentless in her desire for Andrea to follow in her footsteps of total dedication to God as a good Catholic girl. Andrea was therefore enrolled at her church's parochial school as a child and had continued her education entirely in Catholic institutions right up to high school. Her childhood days went on in fairly uneventful succession, under the guidance and tutelage of kind teachers, mostly nuns and sisters of various orders.

Andrea remembered those early days as happy and carefree ones. Attending the colourful, impressive mass on Sundays with her mother and going to other frequent sacred occasions were all exciting highlights for her. She recalled being mesmerized by the priests who dressed in beautifully ornate robes, thinking they were the statues of saints come to life. She believed that they could also hear your prayers and read your thoughts. Above all, she had, and paradoxically still has, an undying admiration for the nuns. She had wanted to become one, much to the delight of her mother.

During the course of several therapy sessions, Andrea's disclosures became increasingly detailed and candid. With minimal interruptions and much encouragement from me, she eventually reached the stage of balanced and confident mental poise that allowed her to overcome the inhibitions that had prevented her from sharing the pain, anger and shame she had been living with for many years.

Her troubles started when she began catechism study in preparation for receiving the important sacrament of First Communion. She was around seven years old at the time and study was conducted by the nuns during Sunday School and catechism classes on Wednesdays.

It was a very special and important event for all the young postulants, and so it was also for little Andrea. When the big day arrived, even the bishop from the big church in the capital city came to visit. Andrea remembers vividly how the children were all neatly lined up in their crisp school uniforms and each would, as they'd been instructed beforehand, ceremoniously walk up and kneel before the bishop and kiss the large ring with the red stone on his hand, after which he would smilingly bless them.

Receiving the blessed sacrament of First Communion was a milestone in Andrea's life. She felt as if her whole being was infused with a rudimentary sense of holiness. She had for the first time received the sacred little wafer from the holy hands of the priest – the little bread that was no longer bread but the body of Jesus entering her body, making her one with Him in holiness.

From that point onwards, Andrea easily progressed into a very private mental dimension of her own, a carefully guarded side to her life and her personality that was so impacting and devastating that her mind had automatically repressed it. By our third therapy session, she was not only recalling but also reliving some abuse-filled episodes of her childhood and pre-teen years that had resulted in troublesome obsessions and compulsions in her life as an adult.

"When I was about nine years old, we went on this trip to Montego Bay. They were taking us to the beach. Father Doherty and Father Simon were with us on the trip, as well as Sister Cecilia and Sister Hope and two other teachers. Father Simon was from Kingston and I didn't know him, but Father Doherty was our priest, the one I grew up with in the church. We were staying over at the school dormitory beside the convent 'till the following day. That's when I found out that several of the other girls and a few of the altar boys were being regularly abused by the priests," Andrea revealed. "It wasn't until years after that I realized how horrible it really was for me, especially on that particular trip. From as early as seven o'clock that night, Sister Hope started sending the children to the other house next door, where the priests were staying, for confession. They would be there for hours at a time. When I was sent over, it was Father Simon who gestured for me to come inside the room. Four candles were burning and one of the altar boys, Damian, was there too. He was one of the bigger boys, about twelve or thirteen years old. He was sitting at a small table drinking something from a cup. It was the red wine, consecrated wine."

She continued: "When I approached Father Simon he looked at me and smiled, then he put his hands on my head and said, '*Welcome my precious little one. I bless you in the name of the Blessed Virgin and her son Jesus. Come over here my little dove, my little nun, come.*' He drew me close to his face and pushed his tongue into my mouth. Then he took a few steps back towards the chair behind him and sat down while still holding my head with his tongue inside my mouth. Then he lifted up his soutanne, the gown. He wasn't wearing anything underneath."

Andrea said Father Simon then used his fingers to close her eyes before removing his tongue from her mouth. He then shoved her head down to his crotch for her to suck his penis.

"While he was doing this, he kept saying, *'My child, your sins are so many. I don't want you to burn in Hell, so I will make sure that your little soul goes to Heaven, to sweet Jesus and the Blessed Virgin.'*"

Andrea said that at the time, she did not feel shy or embarrassed as her mind had been conditioned to be fully obedient to the priest. She went on to describe the feelings she experienced whenever she went to confession. Before entering the confessional booth, a tremor of excitement and anticipation would take hold of her, causing her heart to race and her privates to moisten and throb.

With a wildly palpitating heart, she would part the dark curtains, enter the closet-like, dim enclosure and kneel before the flimsy dividing screen. Her face would be inches away from the priest on the other side of the screen. *'Forgive me, father, for I have sinned,'* she would whisper. The priest would then bless her and soothingly encourage her to disclose all the sins she had committed during the past week.

A few minutes later, he would slide a side panel in the partition dividing the middle cubicle where he was sitting, and Andrea would quietly, totally unobserved, enter his section and perform oral sex on him until he ejaculated. Afterwards, she would quietly return to her part of the booth through the open panel and then go out to one of the nearby pews in the church to kneel and pray. But on one occasion, Father Doherty instructed her to go and sit at the very front pew and wait to be called to do the final part of her penitence with Father Simon.

That was the first time Father Simon sodomized her in the sacristy, the small room beside the altar where the linen, the wine, cups, and other paraphernalia for the mass are kept. It was also Andrea's initiation into what would become a ritual she would suffer almost every week for nearly four years. And even though the priest had applied some kind of a greasy stuff to her anus, it was still very painful for her. At times she would be passed from one priest to another like an object of erotic pleasure, mainly because of her docility, obedience, and apparent enjoyment of the sexual activities. But most of all, it was due to the easy availability of the young girl to the church and the naivety of her foolishly trusting mother.

During our assessment and interviews, Andrea showed signs of psycho-emotional agitation and paranoid thinking with interludes of dissociative symptoms and occasional mental fugue. She revealed that she was regularly assailed by recurrent images and flashback episodes of the countless times she was sexually abused by the priests and later on by their favourite altar boys.

"Doc, do you know that one day, not so long ago, I realized that I could've easily killed him if I wanted to?" she blurted out, laughing at the same time.

"Who are you referring to?" I asked in casual manner, so as not to betray my surprise at her statement.

"It's him I am referring to, Doc, that same old devil, Father Doherty. I used to pass him on the road almost daily as I drive by to classes. Always see him walking down Manchester Road, dressed in his full black as usual, and going towards Saint Paul church. It just came to my mind that one day I would time him and run my car unto the sidewalk and mow him down. Oh, don't worry, Doc. I know that was just a crazy thought. I could never do such a thing," Andrea said. "Even though so much time has passed since, and he is now a very old man, whenever I see him, I get the same feeling of anger and hatred and my heart beats hard, the same way I used to feel every Saturday afternoon before time for confession at church."

The main goal of my sessions with Andrea Newhart was to achieve a corrective emotional experience for her. This is facilitated by the professional stance I have incorporated into my approach which involves being consistently warm, emotionally available, and above all, remaining non-judgmental and supportive at all times. In Andrea's case and many others, where the goal is to alleviate the effects of traumatizing events, it is important for the therapist to be eclectic in his theoretical frame of reference by drawing from different schools of thought, and be flexible in the techniques applied.

It was essential for Andrea to open up about each of those troublesome feelings in a way that would cause her to recover emotionally and behaviourally from the lingering effects of the highly stressful experiences. She was thus encouraged to explore new ways of thinking about her predicament to gain new insights and perceptions on the problem and to overcome the discomfort of talking and thinking about the troubling experiences. For Andrea, a long-lasting obstacle was the underlying fear that things awful and ugly about herself could be revealed and that she might be repelled by these things, rendering her incapable of living with herself because of what she had been through. Andrea's anger was closely attached to a sense of shame manifesting as a relentless internal punishment of the self because she vividly remembered many of those episodes as intensely delightful, though perverse and unsettling for her.

Her experiences were triggers for deep-seated, disturbing emotions. Within the therapeutic setting, the very expression of her emotions was a new, amplified experience for her. We both had, as patient and therapist, gradually developed and shared a kind of personal language, a lexicon of emotion, that fostered interaction and promoted the healing process through an acceptance of self and the experiences, good and bad, that are inevitable parts of that self.

Four months into the therapeutic intervention, Andrea's outlook on life and her optimism about the future took a positive turn, due in part to her natural resilience and the fortitude of character she had acquired. It was also due to her honesty in facing and accepting the experiences she'd lived through, resolutely coming to terms with them.

I also believe that the most important factor that worked in favour of her remarkable progress was her willingness to forgive those who wronged her – the priests for what they did to her and her mother for failing to protect her.

❂

"Doc, one of your students is here to see you. Miss Carla Kamron. Should I send her in now?" the receptionist asked over the intercom.

"Oh yes. No need for her to fill out a personal data form. Just send her in. Thank you," I replied while going through a hefty pile of recently submitted research proposals. Carla came in.

"Have a seat, Carla. Just let me get rid of some of this material here and clear the desk a bit, eh? And how are you doing today?" I asked while shifting some of the papers unto a nearby side table.

"Not too bad, Prof. I want to say thanks for seeing me and giving me some of your time, I know that you're a busy person," she said.

"That's alright. Don't worry. We'll go next door, away from all this distracting stuff here in the office." I had correctly sensed that she needed the soothing surroundings of the therapy room, a setting that would be more inviting.

"Now, Carla, I want you to just relax and make yourself comfortable; take your time and feel free to unburden yourself. Whatever it is, I will do my best to assist you in any way I can. What transpires here is strictly confidential, so, I want you to be as open, candid and frank as you can, okay?"

I patiently allowed her to get used to the ambience – the sound of classical music emanating from discreetly hidden speakers and the smell of jasmine incense. I then persuasively guided her into a state of equipoise, a relaxed harmony of her senses and her mental world that would make it easier for her to share her story.

"Okay, Carla, talk to me. Tell me everything," I said.

"Prof, I don't know how to go about this. Well, what happens is that I've done something wrong, a very bad thing, and I want you to forgive me. I have been dishonest to you and I need your forgiveness. I just cannot keep it any longer. It's bothering me so much that I have been very fearful of saying anything about it because I didn't know how you would react. But afterwards I said, well, I think you will understand and forgive me," she said, speaking in a hushed tone.

"It's alright, Carla, just talk to me. I will understand. I am here to help. I am not only your teacher, but I am also your friend, a genuine friend whom you can trust," I encouraged in a soft whisper.

"Prof, it's about the notebook I said I had left in your office. I deliberately lied to you. I knew that I had it with me all the time. Even when I called you on the phone to ask you about it, I was so nervous and afraid that you might suspect I was lying. I am very sorry."

I remained silent, waiting for her to continue, but she said nothing further. It was as if we were each waiting for the other to break the silence. Two minutes or so later, it had become so unbearable for her that she began speaking again.

"Are you willing to forgive me, sir?" she barely whispered.

"Yes, Carla, I can forgive you as long as you are willing to forgive yourself too and not carry a burden of guilt or shame into tomorrow. No need for you to be too hard on yourself. Of course, you can tell me what caused you to do it, as you said, deliberately," I replied.

"Thank you, sir, but there are other things that you also don't know about. I just didn't have the courage to come out and tell you. Well, the term paper that I submitted with the wrong cover page... I don't know how to say this, Prof, but I also deliberately inserted that cover page. I did it on purpose to get your attention. I don't know where I got the nerve to do such a risky thing because I was taking a chance with my grade since I didn't know how you would react. Prof, I just wanted a chance to talk to you, but I was really too shy to approach you and ask."

"Okay, I understand. But, Carla, it was not necessary at all for you to do that. You could have come to me directly. Surely I wouldn't have turned you away. I even asked if you were having any problems. I am willing to help you," I assured her.

"Well, you said you did all that to get my attention. Now, what I would like is for you to tell me exactly what is bothering you – the problems, the difficulties you're experiencing."

"What happens is that I have no friends, no one I can talk to. I just feel that I can't trust anyone."

She paused. Then, after gathering her thoughts and resolving to open the closed gates of her heart, Carla began a gradual revelation of her inner world, of her sad and gloomy life.

She had for years been living under stressful conditions, experiencing profound emotional instabilities and isolation from family members and people in general. Her mother had long ago migrated to England in search of better opportunities, leaving her in the care of a paternal aunt who strongly disliked her. It was a distressing time in her life as she had to endure not only her aunt's verbal and emotional abuse, but also the sexual and physical abuse from her aunt's boyfriend.

It was during this period in her life, when she was around fifteen, that one of her teachers, Miss Opal, took a special interest in her, assisting her with her school work, school fees and other expenses. After a while, Carla's mother agreed to her leaving her aunt's home to stay with Miss Opal, who lived alone and had no children. Carla was initially very happy living at Miss Opal's home. All her needs were being taken care of, and the teacher was very loving and kind, though she proved to be rather bossy and strict, displaying a very controlling and possessive attitude.

Not long after, Miss Opal, who was about twenty-seven or so, started showing another strange side to her personality. Carla was forced to give Miss Opal frequent full body massages, take baths with her, and even sleep in her bed, often locked in tight embrace with the older woman.

At first Carla saw nothing unusual in all this, and she willingly complied out of a sense of gratitude, but also because she sincerely liked her teacher who was tall, full-bodied, attractive and elegant. But Carla's personal life was soon completely taken over by Miss Opal, who by this time had gradually and cunningly introduced her to blatant acts of lesbian sex, while openly professing an undying love for her.

From then on, the homosexual relationship with her guardian intensified as Miss Opal became increasingly demanding and forceful in her sexualization of the young girl. According to Carla, they had almost nightly bouts of oral sex involving the use of various sex toys for multiple orgasms. Talking to Carla, it became obvious that as a direct consequence of those troubling experiences, she was experiencing low self-esteem, coupled with feelings of helplessness and shame. But our session seemed to reinvigorate her.

Throughout the therapeutic session, I consistently encouraged her to fully disclose her experiences. By so doing, they would soon lose their power to mentally and emotionally enslave her, and she would steadily gain that inner freedom of self, thought and action to which she is fully entitled.

Carla eventually got relief from her sexual bondage under Miss Opal, when the teacher got a government scholarship to further her training in Canada. Though Carla's life had then returned to normal, she was still troubled by the psycho-emotional and functional difficulties that had threatened her chances of enjoying a future marked by a happy and stable marriage, children, family. Carla entered a relationship with a man who, though several years her senior, seemed to genuinely care for her and wanted them to build a life together.

"Mark is a really nice fellow; he's respectful and decent, although a bit older. But he is really in love with me, that much

I know for sure. He loves me much more than I love him. He wants us to get married soon, but I don't know. I haven't told him anything about my past with Opal. Prof, do you think I am a lesbian? I mean, I've told you all about those things that Opal got me into and, you know, I wonder if that is the way I am really," Carla pondered.

Her concerns were real, as the lingering effects of Miss Opal's all-embracing debauchery continued to have a telling effect on her. She was also preoccupied with the thought that she now had a wide vagina, and that Mark, who had a small penis, would be unable to get any satisfaction from sex with her. This worry was an ever present one for her, to the extent that she had to avoid penetrative sex with him.

In clinical practice, we often come across cases of body dysmorphic disorder (BDD), also known as dysmorphophobia, a form of obsessive-compulsive disorder related to anxiety, marked by an individual's persistent preoccupation with an imagined defect in his or her appearance. And if indeed a slight defect is present, the preoccupation with that defect is markedly excessive, sometimes reaching levels of delusional intensity. This constant worry with a physical aspect of appearance often leads to repetitive, intrusive thoughts very similar to the thinking found in persons with obsessive-compulsive disorder (OCD). Although any aspect of physical appearance can become a concern, the most common body part is the face. A patient may complain that his nose is too large, his eyes are not equal in size, his hairline is receding, or that his ear lobes are asymmetrical.

Of course, I was reluctant to immediately arrive at even a pre-diagnosis of BDD with Carla, as I sensed that hers was not just a transitional emotional disturbance or even a delusional expression of poor body image. There was a probability that she could have developed a clinical problem after being physically or sexually assaulted or abused, thereby causing a greater level of self doubt and questioning about the normalcy of her sexual apparatus. Recalling what she had previously mentioned about Miss Opal's penchant for using vibrators, dildos and other sex toys, I decided to revisit that aspect of her sexual experiences with her former teacher.

And indeed, with a little persuasive prodding, she went on to openly and graphically describe the many instances when Opal, while orally stimulating her clitoris and vulva, would also simultaneously insert enormous vibrating dildos into both her vagina and anus, causing her to violently orgasm in endless succession. She felt as if her innards were being stretched to their outmost limit. She further explained that it was only some-time after, during manual self exploration of her privates while using a hand mirror, that she discovered how much her vagina had been distended.

"Carla, I will refer you to a sympathetic female gynaecologist, a specialist in Kingston, who is a good friend of mine, for her to do a thorough examination and assessment. Based on her recommendations, we'll decide how to proceed. The important thing is that the problem can be fixed. I'll discuss it with her first, so don't worry. All will be well," I said. "The other thing is that a sexological examination may be necessary to assess various components of your sexuality such as feeling, arousal, and response patterns. It will also determine whether or not you lubricate well and vasocongest, that is, become erotically swollen and sensitive in and around your vagina. But that would be after the specialist's assessment. That procedure would also help us to answer your question about your sexual orientation, which you seem so worried about. But I do not believe that you are a lesbian," I patiently explained.

In subsequent sessions, Carla was guided into systematic assertiveness training with cognitive reorientation of her locus of control for her to overcome the dysfunctional reality construction that she had been using as a means of explaining the reasons why those negative things happened to her. She went on to gradually acquire the self confidence and love of self that were essential components of her psycho-emotional balance.

I often recall the evening at the annual art fair and exhibition held on the grounds adjacent to the Pastoral Centre. I was admiring an impressive abstract painting when I felt an insistent tap on my shoulder from behind. It took about half-a-minute for me to recognize the beautiful and sexily attired young woman suggestively smiling at me. It was a new Carla Kamron.

She embraced me and went into a showy and confident recital of the empowering self-affirmations I had given her to read and internalize. They had become a part of her life, fuelling her newfound source of inner power, inspiration and supreme confidence.

✿

DAILY SELF AFFIRMATIONS

I AM BEAUTIFUL, I AM ATTRACTIVE, I AM SEDUC-
TIVE,
I AM SPECIAL

I AM STRONG, I AM POWERFUL, I AM WONDERFUL

I AM INVINCIBLE

I WILL BE HAPPY EVERYDAY OF MY LIFE

I WILL MAKE MY DREAMS A REALITY

I AM A WINNER, NO ONE CAN STOP ME

I AM THE GREATEST PERSON EVER

AND SO IT SHALL ALWAYS BE

FOREVER ME

Part Three
The Sublimation

CHAPTER FIVE

The Girl with the Hungry Eyes

"By night on my bed I sought him whom my soul loveth, I sought him, but I found him not."

Song of Solomon 3:1

I had just concluded a therapy session with a young man, a repeat substance abuser who had been diagnosed with multiple sclerosis[13], when Mrs. Ferguson, the administrative assistant at the Medical Centre, signalled for me to take a call. It was my colleague and friend Dr. William Benjamin, who wanted me to rush down to his office, where he had a young lady undergoing a severe panic attack.

I really had no intention of taking on any more assignments that day due to the bad weather conditions brought about by Hurricane Dean, which had pummelled Jamaica's south coast, wreaking havoc on that lush agricultural region. Over in the north coast parish of Saint Ann, we were spared a direct hit but not the incessant rains that pelted the island's flood-prone towns, valleys and plains.

Electricity was off and many roads were turned into streams. It was a miserable state of affairs which most of us took in stride, having grown accustomed to the tropical storms, hurricanes and other natural acts of God which from time to time unleashed their fury upon the island.

Over the phone, it was the uncharacteristic pleading in Dr. Benjamin's voice which not only piqued my curiosity but also made me wonder if there were other unmentioned aspects of the whole matter that prompted him to request my intervention. So I decided to go and see what I could possibly do for his patient. His office was only about four blocks away from the Medical Centre. When I got there, feeling under the weather, the young lady had already been medicated and stabilized and was resting in one of the examination rooms.

"It's one of my new patients, young and educated. She seems to be a decent type. She just walked in showing clear signs of going through a manic crisis or a panic attack. I am more inclined to think in terms of panic disorder, but that's for you to find out in more detail. I told her you're on your way here. She's upstairs. I appreciate you making it through this weather," he said in his signature Tennessee drawl.

"As you see, there's no electricity. We're running on the emergency backup batteries, so there's no AC. I've set up a fan in there. I am concerned about the young miss; she's been uttering some self-destructive thoughts, so it is possible she may be suicidal but I am not sure. That's why I called on you."

I had taken a liking to Dr. Benjamin and his easygoing southern ways. Cool, unhurried, and at times arrogant, he was good at his job. He was trained at the prestigious Howard University medical school in Washington. We both shared an interest in research and in alternative pathways to finding solutions to the many questions and concerns in our respective fields.

"I will see her now, but just for a quick intervention. I will have to do an assessment at any rate. Early next week we can have a formal session. I can't say just yet. Let me check out the situation and then I'll determine what needs to be done," I said.

In most instances, the voicing of suicidal ideas or threats to commit suicide should be taken seriously, even when they're said in a joking or sarcastic manner. Suicidal ideation is most often fuelled by psychic disturbances that yearn for relief, and whenever the individual's distress becomes unbearable, self-destruction presents itself as a solution.

Tracey-Ann Pinto sat timidly before me. It was obvious that she had come in from work, as she was smartly attired in an elegant sky-blue business pants suit which failed to mask her fresh youthfulness; she seemed to be barely out of her teens. Slim and athletically lanky, her body was beginning to take on the voluptuous fullness of a woman. The brief flash of an impish smile from her fleshy mouth made her look like a starry-eyed child savouring a new experience in an endlessly amazing world.

"Are you feeling any better now, Ann?" I asked while carrying out a careful and analytical observation of the non-verbal subtleties she inevitably revealed in the spontaneous projection of her body language.

"Yes, Doc, at least for now. But I know that it's going to wear off, and then I'll be back to square one. It happens all the time," she said, her soft voice sounding as if she was about to break down in tears.

"Okay, just tell me what is distressing you so much. Try to be as frank and open as you can. Everything that transpires here is absolutely confidential, no need to worry. Secrets remain secret.

And even my patient's records are not kept here, they're all in Spanish, and they're encoded and then eventually destroyed. It's the way we do things here to make sure that your private life remains private," I explained in a quiet and reassuring mode, while carefully assessing her every expression, gesture, and revealing aversion of her eyes.

"Well, my problems are so many, Doc. I feel so confused. I don't know what to do. Maybe I take these problems too much to heart. Maybe everybody out there is struggling with even worse problems than mine. I don't know. It's like I can't manage. I just can't cope. At times I feel like just giving up. Everything is a big problem in my life," she said.

"Start by telling me which one is the biggest, most difficult problem for you now, then the next one, number two, and then the other one, number three, and so on. Take your time and just slowly enumerate them, one by one." I was actually guiding her into doing an abstract structuring of those trouble-some things in her mind, putting them in decreasing order, a hierarchy. In order to do this, she would have to manipulate the problems as entities in her mind, as things that can be moved and shifted about, thereby decreasing the emotional impact they have on her.

In addition, that cognitive familiarization or closeness with them would help to reduce the degree of fear and anxiety they generate. She would then be better able to apply analytical, prob-lem-solving approaches to them, which she would not be able to do if she remained emotionally impacted and burdened with fear and anxiety.

"First thing is my memory, Doc. I am losing my memory. I can't remember anything at all, even recent, simple things. Even at work, I am forgetting important steps and procedures. What happens is that I handle money at work, credit card payments, and expense accounts for customers, and at times I can't remember if I just did a transaction or not, or if I issued a receipt or not. I am so worried that I may soon make a serious mistake with people's money." Her silence that followed indicated that she was now about to share problem number two.

"The other big problem is my relationship with my boyfriend; I have lost all feelings for sex, and I don't know, it's like I don't feel for it anymore. I just do it to please him, and I think he suspects that something is wrong with me. I also have a problem with my father and how he treated my mom. Well, they're now divorced, but I am still living at his house," she noted. "Then, I just can't keep any friends, Doc. I think it could be my fault though because I get fed up with them so quickly. It's like I get bored too easily. At times they would be talking to me for a good while and I don't hear a word they say. It's just not registering in my mind. I've been to two doctors already. I got medication, but all it does is quiet me down for a while and make me sleep a lot. But afterwards the problems are still there. They're plaguing my mind. Dr. Benjamin here said he would refer me to you," she added.

"Alright, Miss Pinto. So far there seems to be three major problem areas that need immediate attention, and since they are interconnected, we'll deal with them simultaneously. Then, as other issues emerge, we'll address them one at a time. Now, I want you to know and understand that your situation can be improved as long as you are willing to work diligently towards that desired state of balance, harmony, and wellness. We will begin properly on Tuesday," I said. "Tell me, are you sleeping well? I mean, when you rise, do you feel that you are rested, or still tired with low energy? Yes? Dream often? Okay. And are you able to recall your dreams? Tell me about them, the ones you remember."

I had already detected in Tracey-Ann clear signs of mixed anxiety-depression, which was evident from her clinical presentation. But I also sensed currents of imbalanced psychic energy coming through her aura. I have long since learnt to trust these subtle promptings, for they have proven to be reliable.

"Up to night before last, Doc, I had this dream where I saw myself as a little girl. Well, it was me really and I was dressed up in a pretty white dress in a garden. The little girl is calling me, beckoning with her hand for me to come to her. But I can't hear her voice. It's like I am deaf or something, and I can't move either. And I am looking at myself as a little girl calling to me. Then, suddenly, it is not a garden I am in, but a cemetery, standing between the tombs. It's the second time I've had that dream, and I wonder if it's a sign that I am going to die soon."

She maintained good eye contact while sharing her dream, though her inner preoccupation with the possible ominous significance of the dream clearly shone through.

"Tell me, Miss Pinto, has someone close to you died recently? Like a family member or someone close to you, a friend perhaps? No? Good. Now, we're going to do a little exercise that will help you to relax and gain some calmness, a bit of confidence and self-control. Just relax and concentrate on your breathing. Take rhythmic deep breaths…, not too deep…, right…, take in deep…, let out slowly…again…, good…, yes, good…, now, let your eyes slowly close…, all by themselves…keep breathing, yes, deep in, slowly out," I instructed.

I continued: "You are feeling so light and so relaxed, and now you see a doorway, a dark entrance in front of you with steps going down. Above the entrance you see a word in beautiful gold letters... *Xanadu*..., *Xanadu*..., *Xanadu*. Now, count the steps as you go down the stairway..., one..., two..., three..., four..., five..., six..., slowly, step by step..., you are now going into your inner kingdom..., and you feel so relaxed, so calm, so nice. Another step closer to the seat of your inner power. Relax..., yes, relax. It is so quiet here, so good... *Xanadu*..., *Xanadu*..., *Xanadu*. Yes, breathe. Keep counting the steps... and relax."

I had just applied a modified version of deep relaxation trigger response conditioning (DRTRC), a technique of clinical hypnosis in which a trigger word (*Xanadu* in this instance) is imprinted into her subconscious mind. Later on, whenever she recalls the trigger word she would automatically go into the state of relaxation while remaining fully conscious. On this first occasion for about twenty minutes she was allowed to remain in that state of moderate semi-trance known as twilight sleep, a form of subconsciousness which dulls awareness to pain and makes anxiety less threatening, after which she gradually returned to full consciousness.

"Now, Miss Pinto, whenever you start feeling anxious, confused and sad, frustrated by memory challenges or any distressing emotions, just look at the secret word above the dark entrance. Start taking the steps down the stairway, and you will again become calm, relaxed, and balanced, just as you feel now. Try it, and let me know what happens," I told her. "We will have our first formal session on Tuesday, but in the meantime I would like you to write out an outline of your problems as you see them, your memory difficulties, life with your parents, school, work, a typical encounter with your boyfriend, the sexual difficulties, how you feel about yourself, and so on. Take your time and be as open, explicit, and clear as you can. And don't worry, there's hardly any surprises left in the world for me. I've seen it all. So just write it out in your own words. But it is very important that you start at the earliest time in your life that you can remember."

Two days before the appointed date for Tracey-Ann's therapy session, a plain brown envelope with only my name on it arrived at the office, prominently marked *confidential*. It had no sender's name or return address. It was Tracy-Ann's written life story. It poignantly shared the tale of a youngster troubled by various psycho-emotional disturbances and challenges in her life, while highlighting the circumstances around her that brought them about.

As I read the summary, I felt neither pity nor condemnation for her, only a rare sense of admiration and empathy.

THIS IS ME

Growing up I became detached from the world, always being told that I play too much and that I should go and take up a book. At the time, I was the only child at home, and even though I liked reading a lot, I needed to be among children of my age group who shared similar interests, and so on. My social life at school was alright until I got to grade five.

That summer I was sent to New York for about eight weeks to spend time with my mom, and all I did was watch television and eat greasy fast food, so I got very fat and very uncomfortable with myself. I felt very ugly and it seemed like I was always being made fun of. I also became isolated from everyone in my class. Then at home I was always getting cursed at for one thing and beaten for another; sometimes for very simple things.

It seems like I was a disappointment to my family. My self-esteem was so low that it became clear that I did not belong. I started drifting, not wanting to be part of anything. I was just lost in my faults. At times I would just stare at a single spot on the wall for hours and block out everything else. There was just one thing that I felt happy doing, which was watching television. It was as if I was fully caught up in my own personal world of despair, but I always chose to keep everything that was happening to me bottled up inside. No one knew what was really going on in my mind.

I was never one to participate in class; most times I felt like I was not even there in the classroom. I hated school very much, and the teacher just made it worse by pointing out how quiet I was and how she forgot that I was in the class. I hated her so much for that, and even up to now I still hate her with a passion.

I used to get beaten at school for not doing homework. It was examination time, and we still used to get a lot of

homework that was taken from textbooks that my par-
ents did not bother to get for me. I hated school even
more because of that. My teacher didn't think I would
pass the Common Entrance exam, but I did, and it felt so
good to prove her wrong, especially when I got marks
high enough to get a place at the prestigious Saint
Hilda's High School in Brown's Town.

I was still fat when I got to St. Hilda's, an all-girls
institution. I was miserable, but I was determined to drop
the weight, and as a result I began starving myself. The
other thing is that I had a weak bladder and was in the
habit of keeping up my urine. I had few friends at the
school, but I was doing well academically. Everything
else was pretty much the same – just boring.

I hated my life so much during my high school years that
at nights I would cry myself to sleep and beg God to let
me sleep forever. I just couldn't understand why I was
alive.

By the time I got to grade eight (second form) it became
harder for me to compete against the pupils in my class;
they were the brightest set of eight graders around. I
thought to myself, 'What am I doing in this class.' It sure
didn't feel like a privilege I had worked for, or maybe it
was a mistake on my form teacher's part.

My hormones were intact. I know this because I used to
have strong sexual urges a lot. Sometimes I would think

about what it would be like to have sex with someone, no one in particular at the time. I always enjoyed romance novels and movies that involved kissing. Sometimes I would read hardcore magazines when no one was around.

What really used to get to me was seeing the dogs having sex, especially when they ended up fastened to each other. I remember one day I was sent to the shop to buy something. Down the road, there were about four dogs mating and I just stood there watching them for quite a while. I found it so exciting, and my heart was just pounding away and my privates started jumping on me and got very wet. When I got home my mom asked me why I stayed so long. I told her that there were a lot of people in the shop.

Around that time I started masturbating very often, sometimes up to five or six times a day. I guess I found a lot of comfort in doing it because afterwards I felt better and very sleepy. But it was getting stressful for me as I was afraid that somehow they would find out, especially because I was using things like a banana or a cucumber that I would take out of the fridge.

I would use some Vaseline or hair oil to lubricate my vagina and I would rub my clit while trying to get the cucumber inside me. But after doing this for some weeks, I started worrying that my vagina might be stretched out and not come back to its normal size. I suppose I was angry with myself and trying to hurt myself by doing it.

One day my friend Cassandra showed me a blue movie that her boyfriend left with her. In the movie, I saw the girls using rubber dildos in their bottoms, and as soon as I got home I went into the bathroom and tried it but I didn't like it because at the beginning it hurt. The girls in the blue movie seemed to be enjoying it, so I just couldn't figure out why it didn't work for me.

Mom and dad were having problems. They would fight often, and that made me hate my dad for a while. My mom was so unhappy; she was always crying. She wanted to leave my dad, but she had two of us with him and did not want to leave us like that. I told her that it was okay. I wanted her to be happy.

I was not very close to my family. They didn't seem to understand what was going on. My burdens felt unbearable, and I was always sad. Cassandra, my best friend, was the only person I could trust. I would tell her about the things that I was going through and about my feelings because we were close. I even told her that I felt like I wanted to die.

It was evident after reaching grade nine that my memory had gotten very bad. I found it difficult to remember the things that I was studying, even places I had just recently been to. If I stepped into a store, by the time I was ready to leave I would not know which direction I was coming from. My mind was always straying and racing away, and even those frequent sexual urges that I used to have somehow stopped.

Well, I took the weight off and now I had to worry about being too skinny and too shy. I was just plain uncomfortable with myself. I used to look at other girls and wonder how their figures were so perfect while I just could not get it right. I thought my face, or rather my head, was too big for my body. I have no ass and no curves, and to make matters worse, I felt stupid and out of place.

The thing is, I was oblivious to what was going on in my environment because I did not care. I did not go out and have fun, for I was too self conscious. Watching movies and masturbating was my life. Then I had a friend, this fellow I would talk to, and we used to kiss. But that was it. We rarely saw each other, and after a while I had another boyfriend who tried to get me to have sex with him. He just couldn't understand why I did not want to.

After leaving school, I stopped talking to him because he was never man enough for me. He was always begging money and his aunt had too much say in the way he should live his life. He was nineteen and I was just fed up with him.

I left high school with four subjects, even though it was possible to do better than that. But I was proud of myself because studying was a real hard task for me. I could study the same topic for a whole week, but if the test wasn't right away, I would just forget everything. So, my best strategy was to study the night before exams and get average grades. I then took a year off from full time school and went to evening school instead. I achieved one more subject by this time.

Cassandra and I had plans to go to Brown's Town Community College, but I ended up going to CASE, the College of Agriculture, Science and Education, where I met David, the sweetest, most caring and loving person I had ever known. We became the celebrity couple of the school. Most girls hated me because we were always together, and even my best friend there, Georgia, had a crush on him as well.

My studying strategy remained the same, but this time I had David to encourage me and to help me in areas where I was weak. We would stay up together to study as David was also a last minute studier. The only difference was that he had a quick memory. The bad thing was that he would get impatient with me and my memory problems, as I was really having serious difficulties retaining the course material. Even some ordinary stuff, like everyday routine made me confused.

David became aware of my depression and would try his hardest to comfort me. I had strong attractions towards him, and we would have sex multiple times daily. (You had requested, for the next therapy session, a written outline and details of a typical intimate encounter with my partner, so I am trying my best to be as explicit as possible. I hope that you won't be offended if I am too explicit or if my language is too disrespectful.)

A typical encounter would involve deep kissing from the lips (of which I could not get enough of), and around his neck, stroking his chest while he lay on his back. He would kiss me all over every chance he got, and it was hard for me not to do the same. I became so caught up with him and his body. I used to call him my teddy bear because of his size. But then he convinced himself that he looked fat and dropped a few pounds.

I used to pretend that I was fully into the sex, and David believed it was so. When I would sit on top of him and caress his stomach with my wet pussy, biting him on his neck and on his nipples, he would make all kinds of little sounds and tell me not to stop, or to do that again.

When it became too intense for him, he would grab my waist and position me on top of his dick, and I would ride it until it was inside me. Then he would thrust his dick in and out, and after a while he would stop to give me the lead and we would remain in that position for sometime just moving around and around.

He would be looking straight into my eyes like in a trance, but I just had to look elsewhere, or just close my eyes, because I felt a bit embarrassed while we were doing that. After he climaxed we would kiss and he would hold me close until he fell asleep.

Even though I loved David so very much, I wasn't really enjoying sex at all. I was doing it mainly to please him, faking an orgasm, which to this day, is something I have only heard and read about but never experienced. I became quite good at fooling him about discharging with him at the exact right moment.

It is so funny, Doc, because I would start enjoying it at the beginning, but then just as I become excited and think that I am progressing towards an orgasm, my mind just goes to some other place or time or to some stupid unimportant thing that happened in the past. I would try hard to come back to what we were doing, but the original feeling of excitement was fully lost for me.

Many times after class we would grab our lunch and head for his room – we were boarding students – where we would eat and go for another round of lovemaking, but this time with less kissing as we had to return for afternoon classes. We were always the last to get to class, but we were not hiding anything since everyone knew what was happening.

One time David got real curious and asked me why is it that I never initiated sex with him, and that's when I told him that I did not really like sex. Sex became overbearing for me because I was with someone who was a sex addict and I could not keep up. I was feeling tired and frustrated, and I even suggested to him that he should go and have sex with another girl because I wouldn't mind. He responded by saying that he didn't want anyone to think that they had anything over me and that he could not do that to me.

I understood what he was saying, and I knew why. I was the only girl who ever showed him that I really cared; I wasn't with him for sex, fame or money, but because I cared about him more than anyone else in his life. By the time it got to our second year in school, he began drifting. It was not until school had ended that he made it clear that he really wanted to be in a serious relationship with me.

But I was angry because I felt like he had neglected me for his friends, but nevertheless we stayed together after leaving school. We had been going around for almost four years when I discovered that I was pregnant. I really didn't know what to do. Fortunately, I enjoyed a very good and trusting relationship with my mother, and we could communicate openly and freely. We were more like sisters and friends than mother and daughter.

She was very supportive and helpful. I couldn't let my father know about it. I just knew that he wouldn't understand. I had an abortion. It was a very painful thing for me to do, but living in my dad's house left me no other option. Also, my mother didn't want me to spoil my chances of educational advancement and job opportunities.

I remember saying to myself that I would never again do that because it was really awful. I felt that like something, a real part of me was taken away. The doctor and the nurse both refused to tell me if it was a boy or a girl. According to them, it wouldn't be good for me to know because it would affect me afterwards. I know that it happened because of carelessness or maybe I really did not care. The other thing is that David used to tell me that he was depending on me for regular sex, as he didn't have anyone else, nor was he interested in any other girl.

Although my memory problems seemed to get worse, I managed to get a fairly good job as a front desk receptionist at one of the large hotels here on the north coast. But soon after, I became aware of how serious the problem with my memory failures was. At times, I would be given simple directions to go somewhere, and by the time I get into the car and start driving I forget how to get there, and I have to ask directions or call them on the phone.

My mother went to New York after getting a divorce from my father. I got pregnant again, but this time I decided that I would not hide it from my father. He was very upset when he learned about it. I told him myself, and he responded by saying that if I was going to go through with the pregnancy, I couldn't stay in his house. Furthermore, he didn't like

David at all. I had another abortion. Afterwards, I started taking the pill.

With my boyfriend now, things are not too good. He is very jealous and possessive. He has even grabbed my phone from me and cut off a conversation I was having because he thought I was talking too long on the phone. It can be very embarrassing. Sometimes I feel like it is not working out between us, but it is just so hard to part with him. I have tried a million and one times already. The most recent time was the worst.

(Well, Doc, that's it for now. If I find the time I will continue, but that would be after the next therapy session on Tuesday. Thanks for everything and may God bless you. T.A.P.)

○

Memory dysfunction (episodic amnesia), dysthymia with related abortion remorse depression, generalized lifelong anorgasmia[14]: those were a few of the technical terms on my writing pad that encapsulated Ann's constellation of psycho-emotional problems. Of course, the most serious and difficult to treat was her memory problems because memory pervades every mental and physical function and influences all aspects of our lives.

By the third session, it was determined that her memory difficulties were not in the recall function itself, but rather in the encoding process. She could not recall information or data because they were just not there. Her perceptions were not being sufficiently processed within the short term memory so as to be imprinted in the long-term memory where they would normally be available for recall. Then, her dysthymia, a mood disorder manifesting as a mild form of chronic depression lasting at least two years, in which the person is seldom without symptoms, had also adversely affected her memory function.

"Yes, Doc, that is true, but I never imagined that the dream I told you about could be related to the abortion. I hear people out there talking about this girl that had an abortion and nearly died. She ended up in hospital. They say she is a murderess, and they even call her a walking graveyard and a cemetery, and other terrible names they have for her," she said. "When I hear comments like those it cuts me up inside, but I just try to forget it and move on because, really, there is nothing I can do about it now. I am so sorry it happened that way and I really wish that I didn't have to do it, but it is past and gone."

I could not help but notice how easily and automatically she had reverted to the ego defence mechanism of rationalization, unconsciously calling on the fact that it had already been done and could not be reversed, as sufficient reason to exonerate her. Soon enough she admitted to having experienced transient bouts of sudden anxiety and intense sadness merely at the sight of a mother and small child walking out on the street. For Ann, those were intensely disquieting feelings, which she did not connect to the termination of pregnancy she had opted for.

"Oh yes, Miss Pinto, there *is* something you can do about it, now. Something you *must* do to help you overcome the depressing burden of guilt that you are carrying around and which is also a significant factor in your memory difficulties. You may not be aware of this because it is all happening at the unconscious level, yet its effects are powerful and can be long lasting. It is also likely to be connected to your sexual difficulties," I patiently explained, as she looked at me in puzzled amazement. Then, as I expected, she uttered an inevitable question.

"At this stage, Doc? What could possibly be done now? It's almost two years since I did the termination…, I..," she muttered.

"Ann, listen very carefully. If you should cut off your finger and throw it away, even years after, the fact remains that it was a part of you," I responded. "You need to *speak* to them, to the two children that were not born. Rest your hands on your belly, then face them and express love and a future welcome to both aborted children. Talk to them with all the true emotion that comes from the depth of your heart, just as you would if they were around. Ask for their forgiveness. Know that they have forgiven you, and then welcome them back. Tell them that whenever they choose to return, they will be welcomed, accepted and loved. Seek a quiet moment by yourself and listen to your voice speaking to them. Speak to them truthfully with an open heart. You may not hear an answer then, but you will certainly *feel* it deep within yourself. And most certainly, that will be your healing."

We both remained silent for quite a while, respecting the inner thoughts and feelings of each other. I sensed that in her silence she had made a quiet, almost sacrosanct commitment to bring her unborn children into her life so that her guilt could be lifted and the healing of her inner self could be accomplished.

❁

The next sessions were dedicated to addressing her memory problems and the orgasmic difficulties she had. A series of standard memory tests confirmed a lack of focus and persistent inattention to detail, all of which affected the encoding of data for later recall. She went on to diligently practise the various focus and concentration exercises I had suggested, as well as the mnemonics, those memory aids, mental tricks, and short-cuts-by-association that would help her to recall the essential information (or *engrams*[15]) that should have been imprinted in her mind. The immediate goal was to stimulate and fortify her declarative memory, that part of long-term memory containing factual information, which was at the seat of her recall difficulties in routine and procedural activities, especially when at work.

"Now, Ann, you are still rather young. At twenty-one, you are barely out of your teens, and in many ways you are still growing, still maturing. Sexual climax, the orgasmic release, well, that is something that happens naturally and spontaneously, so you should not try to force it or rush it. Many women experience their first orgasm when they are in their thirties and beyond and have learnt about the responses and capabilities of their bodies," I said. "So, it is not something you work at. Just let it happen on its own, at the right time, the right place, and with the right person, or even with your own self, for some women achieve an orgasm only during masturbation. Others experience it only during oral sex through clitoral stimulation. When you feel pressured to have an orgasm with your partner, and it becomes the goal of intercourse, this could cause performance anxiety which in turn would inhibit sexual arousal and release."

I also told her that her lack of interest in sex and being uncomfortable with her body could have contributed to her depression and anorgasmia.

"This has obviously led to the low self-esteem that is contributing to your lowered sexual satisfaction and the anorgasmia; but in truth and in fact, you do need to emphatically reclaim your sexuality. You will neither be happy or fulfilled without it."

I had taken time to patiently explain in detail, as much as possible, some of the most important features of her psycho-sexual difficulties and their connecting aspects to many of her other problems.

With Ann, the absence of an orgasmic response was primarily due to the lack of excitement and pleasure during sexual activity, a kind of emotional anaesthesia or blunted sensitivity to sensual stimulus. She would require more intense, novel and prolonged stimulation to enter that stage of arousal where she would be mentally, emotionally, and physically prepared and ready for intensely satisfying coitus.

During the therapeutic session, she admitted to having recently developed a love for oral sex. She had first experienced intensely erotic oral sex with an older gentleman, a foreign visitor whom she had met at her workplace. And although there was a repeat episode some three days later, she did not have a truly orgasmic release. She also revealed that her boyfriend had never done it to her.

"Okay, Ann, I trust that you are a good student, because there is some more homework for you to do," I said.

"Um, Doc, why are you always calling me, Ann? My name is Tracey-Ann, remember? Or do I remind you of an Ann that you know?" she asked with a laugh. I found it pleasantly amusing and heartening, as it was the first time since coming to see me that she displayed light-hearted humour and gaiety. It was a very good sign in terms of her recovery and achieving psycho-emotional balance.

"Well, in a way, yes. You remind me of Ann Boleyn, the seventh and last wife of King Henry VIII. I saw a film entitled *Ann of the Thousand Days*, which is based on her life story. That was very long ago, though," I said.

"But, Doc, that's terrible of you to compare me to her. Isn't she the one who was beheaded by orders of her very husband, the King, just as he did with his previous wives when he got tired of them, eh?" she asked.

"Ahh, but your memory seems to be clicking quite alright, young lady. Yes, that's true. Of course, it doesn't mean that you'll end up like her, decapitated for treason. Make sure you don't marry into royalty though, just to be on the safe side, eh?"

We both laughed at the easy jovial banter that flowed smoothly between us.

"Okay, Miss Tracey-Ann, you really need to get to know your true self intimately and fully so as to overcome all the negative conditioning, the limiting attitudes, and other obstacles that have been hindering your enjoyment of sex. There are certain exercises and various procedures we call sensory exploration, or sensate focus, that can help amplify your body responses," I said.

"This is something you will practise all by yourself in the privacy of your bedroom, with scented candles and soft music if you like. You will learn to respond erotically with all areas of your body, sort of awakening all your body cells to erotic stimulation. It involves body exploration, genital self-examination, and sexual fantasies with erotic guided imagery. It is easy and most enjoyable, once you learn the techniques of self-pleasuring."

After a few more instructionals, I handed her a standardized list of tips that would help her to complete the assignment. It went something like this:

<u>Therapy and Enrichment for Orgasmic Difficulties</u>

Place yourself in a situation conducive to getting sexually aroused.

Begin by touching parts of your body that feel arousing.

Feel your body and slowly explore it with your hands. Look at your body alone in detail and use a mirror to inspect your genitals.

Learn to give yourself an orgasm through masturbation. Be patient.

Include sexual fantasies in your masturbatory therapy. Move your body in ways that give you the best stimulation.

Focus on sexual feelings and continue the sensate focus techniques.

Tighten your legs and thighs to increase muscle tension which helps to trigger orgasm.

Do the Kegel exercises[16] you've been taught, as often as you can.

Try using a vibrator or dildo to help achieve your first orgasm.

After you have developed some skill in the erotic awakening of your body, your partner can participate in the exercise, but avoid penile-vaginal intercourse at first. Follow these other tips and suggestions:

Have your partner watch you masturbate. Then imitate you.

Experiment with oral stimulation, manual stimulation, body rubbing and sensuous massage.

Use the "woman on top" sexual position for better control.

With your partner, view erotic/pornographic films.

Integrate a dildo/vibrator into lovemaking. Be careful not to rely on it exclusively, as this may decrease your ability to fantasize and may cause jealousy or resentment from your partner if they are unable to satisfy you without a dildo/vibrator.

❂

"Excuse me, Doc, your client is here. The American lady who was referred by the law office. Oh, and Miss Pinto has not shown up for the second time. She didn't come last week either. Maybe I could give her a call. Yes, sir, her appointment was for three o'clock."

Mrs. Ferguson, our pleasant administrator and receptionist, had by now developed a high level of smooth proficiency in the handling of patients and clients for two general practitioners and the adjacent counselling unit. She claimed that the task was made more demanding by *my* clients, with all their strange and highly unusual behaviour.

Terri Adamson was your average visitor from North America, who had for years eagerly salivated at the prospects of sampling Jamaica's renowned triad of sun, sea and sex that her friends back home had luridly told her about. In her eyes, Jamaica was the tropical paradise where her hottest erotic fantasies, and more, could be easily fulfilled. Terri was an attractive, unmarried blonde Bostonian socialite in her late thirties. She had somehow fallen under the influence of some unsavoury local characters: pimps and drug pushers, who wasted no time in exploiting her to the hilt, in every possible way. She had been persuaded by them to extend her stay in the island as she fully imbibed the local subculture of drugs, promiscuous sex and hedonistic, carefree lifestyle.

During the first five months or so, things were fine as she was able to freely indulge her cravings which she could not openly express back home. She'd had a staid and conservative upbringing, but she had a rebellious and adventurous streak. Her parents had always exhibited some level of racism and would never let their little girl mix or even socialize with non-whites, Latinos, Jews, or God forbid, Black men. But, from her early teens, Terri had developed a curious, almost fetishist attraction towards Black men.

The attorney's office nearby had sent her over as she was in a very agitated state, confused, nervous and unable to decide whether she wanted her Jamaican boyfriend arrested or have a restraining court order issued against him. He had, for the umpteenth time, roughed her up and slapped her around in front of his friends apparently for no reason but to show off his total control over her.

"I don't want Denton to be locked up in jail or anything like that. I love him and I know that he loves me too, but it's just his temper. He can be so aggressive towards me at times that I just wonder if I am doing the right thing. He knows that I love him and I have proven it to him in so many ways..., I... I just want...oh God..," she said before breaking down in tears, her eye shadow and mascara streaming like mini-rivulets down her cheeks.

I handed her facial tissue and waited a few moments for her to delicately daub her tears. She clearly needed to be stabilized first to bring her agitated emotions into a state of quiescence. After ensuring that she was comfortably seated, breathing rhythmically and poised for relaxation, I started guiding her into a desired state of mind-body equipoise.

"Now, Terri, I want you to bring the thoughts and distressing memories of it all into your mind right now. Okay, now I want you to focus on your feelings, on the unpleasant emotions you are experiencing right now. Yes, good. Try to identify and explore the unsettling feelings, those unpleasant emotions. Just be aware of those feelings. Tell me, where do you feel them mostly? In your stomach, eh? Okay. Now, place your hands on your belly and follow your breathing, track your breathing with your hands. Just feel your breathing through your hands, and track and follow the pattern of your breathing…good…, very good. Keep at it just like that…, good. Alright, tell me how you feel now," I instructed.

"I feel lighter, and my heart is not racing away. I just started feeling a little bit calmer," Terri said.

"What would you like me to do for you, Terri?" My question was a rhetorical one, for I already knew that what she was subconsciously seeking was a comforting reassurance and some kind of accommodating arrangement whereby she can remain with the abusive man, but with a false sense of personal security coming from the law.

"Someone has to speak to Denton, Doc, to let him understand and realize that I am only trying to do my best for him, and it is unfair for him to treat me like this. He has no reason to complain about me. I've been a good woman to him. There's nothing I wouldn't do for him, but it's disgraceful the way he treats me at times, humiliating me in front of his friends. He just tells me whatever comes to his mouth," Terri explained. "Three months ago, I bought him a car that he uses as a taxi, and I still have to give him money to service it and money for gas. This man is so heartless, Doc. I am also providing for his baby and his babymother, and I've never once complained about it. He knows I am doing it just because of him. It is so painful for me. They just don't seem to understand," she added.

A submissive-dependent personality with latent masochistic tendencies and low self esteem were among the terms I jotted on my writing pad. Terri Adamson was also worried about being single, of not having "a man of her own". And so, regardless of the demeaning and humiliating treatment from Denton, she stayed with him, her domineering and unruly stud.

In a later session, we uncovered the source of Terri's rather uncommon form of obsessive fixation with certain types of black men. Certain smells always had an effect on her which she couldn't explain or resist. In analyzing the dynamics of her poor and reckless choices in the many dysfunctional relationships she had entered, it became obvious that she always gravitated towards burly black men.

She gradually, though reluctantly, came to recognize that she had somehow developed a sexual attraction to the musky smell of male perspiration and sebum. The pheromones in the excretion of certain men, especially muscular and heavily built black guys, were intoxicating and erotically stimulating and hard to resist. It also made her vulnerable to abuse and exploitation when her submissive disposition became obvious to unstable and insecure ones like her precious Denton.

We applied a multimodal therapeutic approach for Terri that involved techniques of clinical hypnosis, aromatherapy, and breathing meditation to address her olfactory-sexual fixation. We also did some cognitive restructuring to deal with the maladaptive pattern of negative life choices she had cultivated for so long and which had plunged her into the sorry situation she was now in.

With assistance from the attorney's office and the American consular representatives, Terri managed to eventually extricate herself from the bad relationship with Denton. Not long after, Terri packed her things and left Jamaica, vowing never to return.

○

The moment she entered the office, I knew that something had happened, something good. Tracey-Ann was casually dressed in shorts, a halter top mini blouse, tennis shoes, and carrying a backpack with her laptop computer in it. But this time she was smiling broadly. Her eyes glowed with bubbly and youthful mischief.

"I am here for my session, Doc. It's my day off, that's why I am dressed like this. It's hot out there. You're going to strangle me, Doc. I haven't been able to do all the exercises. I just don't have the time. But I did the erotic mapping and the Kegel exercises. They're good," she said.

"Miss Pinto, it is so good to see you. You are surely looking great. Let's hope it's both inside as well as outside. I am happy that you at least managed to do those," I replied. "Wait a minute, let me guess. It came, right? I mean, your orgasm, it came at last? Well, great, that's fantastic! Wow! Congratulations! It makes *me* feel good too. Okay, Ann, now just relax and give me some details about that experience." She was happy and I was happy for her.

"That older gentleman I told you about, Doc, he is from Ohio. He is a wonderful person. He's a big man though, old enough to, well, be my father. Anyway, he invited me and my co-worker Marcia out to dinner three days ago. He flew back home yesterday but promised to return in December. He is a mortician and owns a large funeral home there. He fascinated us with stories about the funeral business and embalming of bodies and so on. But my friend Marcia told me that she noticed how even while he was talking, it was obvious that he was fully interested in me alone," Terri said.

"We all laughed when I asked him if he ever looked into the eyes of the corpses at the funeral home. Then he got serious and said, *'No, never. But I sure could get lost in your eyes.'* Anyway, later that evening he asked me, and I spent the night at his apartment. We had oral sex, and this time, well, I don't know how to say it, but I am sure I climaxed at least three times in all. It was unbelievable, Doc. I felt like my whole body was vibrating. For a while, I thought I was going to die. But we didn't have intercourse at all. I didn't want to go that far because of David, my boyfriend. I didn't want it on my conscience that I cheated on him," she explained.

"Have you any regrets at all about the experience? Anything that you feel uneasy about, or that may be bothering you?" I asked.

"No, Doc, I don't think so. As a matter of fact, I was never totally naked with Mr. Lambert. In the beginning I was slightly nervous, and he said that he would give me an 'XTC' to relax. Everything went very well. It was fabulous. We even had champagne; it made me feel like I was floating away, like on air bubbles. Even though we didn't have full sex, I did ask him about using a condom, and you know what he said? He said that using a condom was like taking a shower while wearing a raincoat," Ann said.

"Well, your elderly gentleman from Ohio is certainly well-experienced. Oh yes, the champagne alone wouldn't give you that air bubbles, floating-away sensation. That was from the 'XTC'. That's the slang term for the designer drug ecstasy. Most likely it was in your champagne. It gives you a flushed, sexual euphoria. It acts like a hallucinogen but without the hallucinations. It also removes communication barriers, lowers inhibitions, and even reduces normal fear response. It is potentially dangerous if used carelessly," I said. "I would advise you to be extremely cautious when in the company of these visitors, the elderly gentleman type. They can turn out to be very deceptive," I added. Ann gave out a throaty, hearty laugh, promising to be more prudent and careful in such situations in the future.

"Well, it's just a little over two weeks since your last session, Ann. Do you remember what I was wearing the last time we met?" I pointedly asked. I was pleased to hear her give an accurate and rather detailed answer.

"Okay. And how many persons were outside in the waiting hall when you came in today? Very good. How many men and how many women? Excellent! And the receptionist, Mrs. Ferguson, what is she wearing today? Well, no, not exactly. Not a white blouse this time. Don't guess. Okay, please go outside and take a discreet look."

She returned in less than a minute, triumphantly exclaiming, "But, Doc, it is *your* memory that seems to be failing, because right now she *is* wearing a white blouse, just as I told you!"

"Yes, you are right; but you were not certain of your answer a while ago. Anyway, that was fairly good. Please continue the focus and concentration exercises. Use the mnemonics short cuts and the little association pictures you are to attach to people's faces, names, and so on. Just don't neglect any of the instructions I gave you, okay? Good. How is your dream world coming on? And the fantasies, are they any different or more frequent?" I asked.

"Well, Doc, let me tell you. I haven't had any of those disturbing dreams at all, especially since I started taking that herbal tea you told me about. I am sleeping much better now, but I am really having some real way out fantasies. I mean, in the day when I am fully awake, they would come into my mind, totally unexpected. Sometimes I just laugh out loud, and folks who happen to be around at that time would look at me as if something was wrong."

"Describe those fantasies, Ann, and tell me how you feel about them," I instructed.

"Ah well, they are really weird, Doc. I've never really put my mind to anything like that before. I remember on Sunday I was all alone at home just relaxing, listening to some music, when all of a sudden I started seeing myself having sex with two men at the same time. It was so real, like it was actually taking place at that moment. Then a girl I didn't recognize came and started caressing and kissing me while these two guys were making love to me. Is that a normal thing, Doc?"

"Having erotic fantasies is quite normal and healthy too. Actually living out those fantasies can be risky. How often are you experiencing these fantasies, Ann?"

"Not too often. Like once or twice in a day, especially when I am relaxed and my mind is not on anything in particular. You know what, Doc? At times I wonder what it would be like to be a porn star, to be in one of those blue movies…, ha, ha, ha!! But I don't think I could ever do it. I don't know how those girls get the courage to do those things on camera," she explained, interspersing her answer with giggles and coyness.

"Okay, there's another thing, Ann, and this is very important. I know how you feel about your father and your mom, and his attitude towards you and David and so on. But you need to come to terms with that situation to forgive him and fully restore a healthy relationship between you both in a similar way to how you dealt with the children that were not born. You are to take the initiative, approach him with love and forgiveness in your heart, and talk to him as a daughter without recriminations or past bitterness. Express your love to him and invite him to start anew, to open a new chapter in the book of your lives. He won't reject you once he senses the sincerity and the love in your heart towards him," I said. "You see, what happens is that there is a certain subtle but very forceful dynamic within a family unit, a kind of invisible bond that creates tension when it becomes fragmented, broken, or crushed. This can make you ill mentally, physically and spiritually too. Folks here in Jamaica have a true saying, and you must have heard it. They say that blood is thicker than water. We all experience, sooner or later in our lives, that mysterious, magnetic pull of the family blood. It is something we must respect. Without that restoration, your healing will not be complete, Ann."

Ann remained silent for a few moments, with eyes closed. Then she looked at me with tears in her eyes and softly said, "Thank you, Doc. I thank you so much for encouraging me to do that, to forgive my father. I know it's the right thing to do, and I will do it. I surely will. I have always wanted to because deep down I do love my dad."

❁

CHAPTER SIX

The Girl with the Narrow Hips

"For the lips of a strange woman drip as a honeycomb, and her mouth is smoother than oil. But her end is bitter as wormwood and sharp as a two-edged sword."

Proverbs 5:3-4

"Hello, good morning, Doc. Sorry to call you so early. I gave a lady your mobile number. She will call you soon. She insisted that she wanted to talk to you personally before making an appointment. I know that it is not the proper procedure, but she sounded so desperate and nervous. Her name is Lisa Nicola Bryant. No, sir, she did not leave a telephone number. No, she didn't want to give any information at all. She said she needs to see you urgently," said Mrs. Ferguson over the phone.

"Well, fine, that's alright. Excuse me just a minute please, Mrs. Ferguson. Oh yes, it is her. It's Mrs. Bryant. She is on the other line right now thank you. We'll talk later on. Yes? ... Oh, hello Mrs. Bryant."

"Good morning, Doctor. I called your office and the assistant gave me your number. I need to see you as soon as possible; I am really going through living hell. I don't think I can manage any longer. I think I am going crazy, and I've been to several doctors already. Doc, sorry but, are you an Indian? Your accent..., I...," It was a nervous, confused, almost incoherent voice on the line. I however, immediately sensed that it came from an educated, cultivated and refined lady who was undergoing some profoundly distressing life experiences.

"Oh no, my background is more Spanish. Well, Latin American really. Can you come in day after tomorrow, Friday..., say at around three in the afternoon?" I asked.

"Yes, sir, that is okay with me. You know, Doc, I was raped at gunpoint and everybody, even my mother, has turned against me. They are like barracudas. I need to get away from their clutches. I have no one to turn to," she said. The hurried staccato of her rapid fire chatter caught me almost off guard.

"Okay, I hear you, Mrs. Bryant, but when we meet on Friday we'll examine everything in depth and we will try to help you to the best of our ability. But right now I would like you to practice breathing deeply and slowly. Take at least six deep breaths with your eyes closed, concentrating on your breathing whenever you feel distressed, confused, or when any disturbing thoughts or memories come to your mind. It's simple and very easy, and it will help you to calm down and feel a little better. Will you try that, Mrs. Bryant?"

"Well yes, I can try that, Doc," she responded.

"Good. When you close your eyes, just try to visualize the picture of a beautiful, peaceful blue lake, surrounded by round hills with flowers and trees and singing birds, and you are right there relaxing and taking in the lovely scenery. Continue breathing deeply and rhythmically for a while. Try that, and don't worry. We'll see you on Friday, so until then, do take good care of yourself." I ended the conversation on that note though it was obvious that she would've preferred to continue talking on the phone.

A few days later when she walked into the office, immaculately dressed and flawlessly put together in an exquisitely designed Escada outfit, she was the eye-catching picture of loveliness and cosmopolitan elegance. Tall and slender, her recently coiffed chestnut brown hair and appealing oval face suggested Spanish-Mediterranean roots. Mrs. Lisa Nicola Bryant was well aware of the arresting visual impact of her physical presence. It was an asset she often used to personal advantage, especially within the local hospitality industry, where over the years she had succeeded in securing various mid-level management positions though she was never able to keep them for long.

Superficially, at first blush, she would easily give the impression of being a fully balanced, attractive and polished lady of high status in life. Yet, beneath the urbane veneer of cultured, lady-like civility I could not help but perceive a subtle raunchiness in her persona, a kind of angry, repressed sensuality that was betrayed by a suggestive, libertine glint in her eyes. It was just a certain look that came across as impudent insouciance. It was a peculiar, openly defiant look I had often seen in those who are afflicted by various forms of risk-taking addictions.

Lisa had for quite a while now been assailed by a heavy burden of complex psycho emotional problems, manifesting as a profoundly distressing, soul tearing anguish that had seriously affected her marital and family relationship as well as her occupational and wider social interactions. How deep and extensive these were, became evident as the harrowing psychodrama of her tumultuous life gradually unfolded.

"My sleeping pattern? Well, that is totally way out, Doc. I would go to bed at around ten or eleven and by two or three in the morning I am fully awake again and can't go back to sleep. I would just be there in bed, with all kind of weird thoughts in my mind. I would turn on the cable television, and it would be on and I am looking at it but not taking in anything at all, like everything is just going right through me. I would watch for hours until I manage to fall asleep, then I am awake again.

"Oh, I've stopped taking those pills, even though they help me to fall asleep. I am not going to be on any damned pills for the rest of my life. That's ridiculous. I mean, really now, I'm not a junkie to be on pills forever," she said. Very articulate and rather loquacious, she seemed to have a way with words, something which I later to found out was her devastating means of lashing out at anyone who dared to offend her, whether real or imagined.

"Mrs. Bryant, I would like you to describe those weird thoughts that come into your mind during the early morning hours when you are unable to go back to sleep. Try to recapture and carefully explore your feelings and the emotions you experience at that time while you are awake."

"Well, it's like I am constantly looking back, like going over and over every little incident, every little thing that happens in my life, and how these people I am around are so bitchy, so evil and treacherous. I feel that I am losing out on life, Doc. It's like life is passing me by. I mean, a woman like me. I feel like I am a prisoner in that house we're living at now; it is his mother's house, that's my mother-in-law. And then his two brothers also live just next door, and they all hate me for no reason at all. They're so ungrateful, after all I've done for them," Lisa explained.

"Well, I spend most of the time inside the house. I don't even want to see any of them, and my husband is always on their side, he doesn't defend me at all. I feel like I am stuck with this man. We've been married for four years now, but we have been together on and off for twelve years in all. I have left him three times already, but I always end up coming back to him. It's like I feel sorry for him. I've been with Carl from I was eighteen."

Lisa continued: "I am thirty one now, Doc. No, we don't have any children, although he has a son with another woman, a dim-witted, idiotic, horse-faced hustler that trapped him good and proper, but that's another story. And it is not even his real son, but he thinks the child is his. Can you imagine that my mother, my own mother is on his side? Even now he has her totally fooled. She thinks I am to be blamed for everything. She sides with him, always telling me to calm down and be reasonable.

"He wants to have children, but I always tell him that I don't think we are ready for that, even after all this time. My mother, too, would like to see me bloated and pregnant as long as she gets her precious little grandchildren to show off. She doesn't really care about me. The truth is that I don't want to have children with him. And, anyway, long ago I decided I would not have any children so as not to feel the belly cramps and the pain of poor mothers out there, seeing their children suffering, abused and even slaughtered daily. Right, Doc? Right?" she insisted while staring me down, her dark eyes filled with tension.

"No, I don't think so, Mrs. Bryant. Not having children of your own will not shield you from being torn up deep inside, because you will still feel the pain when you see the anguish of despair, the sorrow in other women, other mothers, for we are all one, and we do experience deep down the pain of others, although in a vicarious way. But tell me, how long now have you been experiencing the anxiety, the distress and the sleep disturbances?" I asked.

"It's been over five years. Five long years. Everything just started to go down and down for me ever since that incident I mentioned the other day. I was raped by two guys, two criminals, and up to this day I have no idea who they are. Well, nobody knows. The police did their best. But it is really because of that so-called husband I have; he is a wimp and a coward, and I've told him that many times to his face. How can I know that I am not passing by those rapists out there in the street somewhere and don't even suspect it is them? But they would surely know me, and for all I know those bastards might even be laughing at me right now. Why does a man rape a woman or a young girl, Doc? Can he get any real pleasure when it is against her will, and the person is so scared and terrified? They must be sick." Lisa trailed off into a brief silence, covering her face with both hands, not allowing herself to weep, but maintaining her steady poise through sheer inner strength.

"Most definitely, rape is a terrible ordeal for any woman, especially because rapists often inflict more violence on their victims than is necessary to achieve their goals. Many of them are not really sick in the usual sense, and rape is not a sexual disorder either; it is a serious crime that is not primarily a sexual act but rather an act of brutality and aggression. The basic motivation is usually to attack, humiliate, subordinate, and degrade the victim, and to exercise total domination over them", I said.

"It must have been devastating and very painful for you, Mrs. Bryant. And although you must have spoken about it several times over, I would really like you to share your story with me. Walk me through it, but from a different perspective this time – *not* as a victim, but as a *survivor*. Yes, you have survived, with painful and lingering problems, but you can overcome them and go on to live a good life. I will try to help you as much as I possibly can. Now tell me what happened. Just tell me in your own words."

The memory of the terrifying experience was so indelibly etched in Lisa's mind that the mere evocation of it would invariably cause her to vividly relive the heart-pounding ordeal.

Though not married at the time, Lisa and Carl had decided to move into a rather small apartment building with only twelve studio units, located at the end of a lonely dead-end access road in a new, developing suburb. It was inexpensive, and at that time they also had a vehicle for their convenience. The whole compound was fenced around, and the owner occupied one of the ground floor apartments. He also kept dogs which were let out at night. But on this particular night the owner was away and had instructed the gardener to keep the dogs locked in their kennels.

At about ten o'clock that night, as she was in bed with her husband, totally nude and engaged in vigorous sexual intercourse, she glimpsed the shadow of a person at the front window, looking in at them. Before she could say anything to alert her partner, the door was kicked in by a man with a gun in his hand. He was wearing only bath trunks and his face was covered by a diving mask.

After roughly ordering them to be silent, he demanded money which they didn't have, then jewels, which Lisa hurriedly gave him. He then threatened to shoot her husband, but she pleaded with the assailant, who ordered Carl to go under the bed and remain silent. Then another man came in, and her heart sank even more when she saw him. He had a ladies' stocking covering his head and face, and a gleaming ratchet knife in his hand. But this guy was totally calm and in no hurry and had a giggle-like laughter that came out a bit muffled through the stocking.

He searched around the tiny apartment for a few minutes, pulling out drawers at random and throwing things around after which he just casually went over to the terrified Lisa Nicola, dragged her unto the bed and slid down his shorts. When she told him that she had condoms in the night table draw, he laughed and asked if she thought he had a disease or something. The other fellow kept the gun pointed at her, then, when his turn came, he passed the weapon to his accomplice who again kept it trained on her.

It became obvious that while describing the whole traumatic experience, Lisa was experiencing significant levels of suppressed emotional agony, a form of subjective pain with strong similarities to physical pain which she was able to enshroud and contain within herself. But over time, this unsettled emotion had crystallized into seething anger, mainly because a long time had passed during which she had to live with the shame and the disturbing knowledge that the unknown rapists may be neighbours, residents, workers, or people who may know and see her daily. This reactive frustration was the true source of her unremitting, chronic, treatment-resistant depression. Denied an identifiable target by not knowing who carried out the sexual assault on her, she wantonly lashed out at those near her including friends, family, and foes.

She knew that she had survived the extended rape without any major physical injuries, and according to her, she had also saved her hubby's life in the process because of her total co-operation with those brutes. She realised that the rapists knew her, or maybe had been watching them, studying their movements for sometime, but were obviously low class, and so would've never dared to approach her in any normal social circumstance.

It was clear to Lisa that the men had good knowledge of the usual routine around the apartment complex, for they carried out their actions slowly, using her in every which way, vaginal, anal and orally. At times both of them simultaneously abused her while spewing out all manner of foul obscenities and humiliating remarks at her husband cowering under the bed.

Much later, as they were about to leave, the one with the stocking mask turned around, grabbed her by an arm and began pulling her away towards the door. With her free hand she managed to remove the sheet from the bed and covered herself with it, at the same time unwittingly covering the man's arm around her waist with the knife's cold metal resting on her navel. They calmly walked her towards the gate which was still unlocked. Then the fellow with the knife casually said, "*Hey gal, you good, you know. Ah long time me ah admire you. Me soon come check you again so just cool, alright?*" With that outrageously brazen remark he eased her away from beside him, and they swiftly disappeared into the nearby darkness of the thick surrounding bush.

Lisa said she hurried back to the apartment, feeling the painful soreness, the internal bruises, and the leaking semen trickling down her inner leg. Carl Anthony was still under the bed, trembling with intense fear. It took a while for her to convince him that it was safe for him to come out as the men had finally left. Resisting the temptation to take a shower and to douche, she called the police and reported the crime. After loudly berating and insulting Carl for not having the guts to even call the cops while she had been taken away by the attackers, she decided not to wait for the lawmen but instead drove herself, alone, to the nearby police station. The lengthy and frustrating investigation into the crime petered out after a while as no suspect was ever identified.

❁

"As you mentioned during our last session, Lisa, it bothers you greatly that those guys seem to have gotten away with their terrible deed. And surely what makes it even worse is that they remain anonymous, faceless figures in your mind. That makes it very difficult for you to kind of get a mental grasp on them; they are like shadows, eh? So you would spend a lot of time turning all kind of possibilities over and over in your mind, guessing and speculating as to who it could be, and so on, right?"

"Well, yes, Doc, that's true. The problem is that I am constantly suspecting whether it could be this man or that one. At one time I was strongly suspecting the mechanic at a garage we take the car to sometimes. Maybe it's because he's always making passes at me, you know, like how I look so good and that kind of foolishness men always say to every woman they see out there. It was long after that I realized it could not be him; his voice just didn't fit any of the rapists. Same thing went on for a while with this other man who used to work at the golf club, and would at times also do odd jobs around the house for my mother. Similarly, after a while it dawned on me that he would be much older than any of them, so it could not be him either, and so on."

The exasperation, confusion, and frustration Lisa had been grappling with were evident even as she revisited the private terror she had lived through and the unending, distressful consequences she was unable to overcome.

"Now, Mrs. Bryant, before we go on to the therapeutic approach we have designed for you, and which I will explain to you shortly, I would like you to consider this for a while, then tell me what comes to your mind. Suppose those fellows are caught and brought before you for you to punish them yourself, what would you want done to them?"

"Done to them, Doc? What are you really saying to me? I myself would do it. I would put them into a wooden shack and nail their testicles to the wall, then light the shack afire. No, no, wait a minute, that would be too swift, too quick for them. I want them to suffer long and hard, so I just need a bottle of log-wood honey and I would tie them up both on an ants nest and pour the honey on them. I would watch them for days while they are eaten up by the ants," she replied.

"Think you'd feel good after that? I mean, good within yourself, Lisa," I asked.

"It would be my greatest joy to see them suffering to the max, Doc. I am sure of that." Her answer was marked by fiery passion mixed with an intense desire for revenge.

Following the rape ordeal, Lisa suffered a break from reality and a breakdown in the coordination of thoughts, actions and emotions. She felt hopeless, helpless, and off balance, and saved from going totally insane only by the solicitous care of her mother and the welcome oblivion afforded by the heavy sedation she had been placed under by their family physician.

She separated from Carl Anthony and went to stay with her mother for a short while before travelling to the United States to stay with relatives and undergo further treatment. Having recovered physically, but with significant residual psychological and emotional problems, she fell into a pattern of self-destructive behaviour, such as openly rebellious promiscuity, indulging in wanton, opportunistic sex with numerous strange, anonymous men whom she met at singles bars and nightclubs. She also started smoking heavily both tobacco and marijuana.

Lisa admitted during therapy that it was the result of her intense anger turned inwards and eating at her heart. And although some years had passed since undergoing that critical phase of her slow return to normalcy, she never achieved a level of complete stability, but was constantly grappling with various mental and emotional disturbances that waxed and waned in their severity and intensity.

A process of differential diagnosis, to merely assist in guiding our analysis, revealed consistent signs of paranoid psychosis (delusions of persecution), chronic unremitting depression[17] and a diffused form of generalized anxiety disorder[18] (GAD).

I quickly realised, however, that her clinical picture was one that presented special challenges, such as the overlapping and at times obscure symptom profile, as well as the sheer complexity of her unique personality makeup. And surely, soon after, we also had to seriously consider the combination of at least two personality disorders – narcissistic[19] and borderline[20] – to her already complex presentation.

By her third session, we had already gone through several procedures such as the Social Readjustment Rating Scale to help us determine her level of accumulated stress from significant life events, the free word association to probe for disturbing, subconscious repressed entities. We also used the expanded Rorschak and Thematic Apperception Test. But then, just as I feared, everything seemed to point towards personality traits that had been exacerbated to breaking point by the severely distressing events and life circumstances Lisa had been through.

"Lisa, so far we have gone through various stages of the therapeutic approach for your situation, and you had previously also been through other methods with my distinguished colleagues whom you had consulted. Well, I believe you would benefit greatly from an entirely different process; it is a departure from the usual psychotherapeutic orientation. But in my clinical experience, when applied correctly, it works wonderfully. Let me briefly explain what it is about. I will try to make it as simple and easy to understand as possible," I said. "You might have heard the common saying out there about trying to keep body and soul together. Yes? Well, there is an underlying truth in that. There is really no separation or division between mind and body; they are *one*. Our mind is infused into each and every cell of our physical body, but body and mind must be in harmony with each other. They must be balanced for us to function effectively and be able to face problems, challenges, threats and danger without being overwhelmed."

"Yes, Doc, I know what you mean. Like me going wacko, crazy and, what you call it? Insane, a lunatic, ha, ha, ha. That's why I've ended up going to all you shrinkheads over the years. Oh, and by the way, my mom says she wants to talk to you. I don't know, but she may want you to send me to the madhouse, have me admitted. I wouldn't be surprised; they all want to get me out of their way, out of their sight. And Carl Anthony, well, he has agreed to consult with you," she said. "He's so devious and cunning. I'm sure he has something up his sleeve, but I think he needs the counselling and the therapy even more than I do. He just gets on my nerves. I can't stand him. Both he and my mom are constantly plotting against me," Lisa said, rolling her eyes then smiling at me.

"Sure, I think it would be a good idea for Carl to come in. We could have an extended session next week with you both. Just give your mother my phone number and ask her to call me, then we'll take it from there, okay? Good. Now, tell me Lisa, have you ever heard of the *chakras* or the *kundalini*? No? Well, those are really ancient Hindu terms, but the chakras refers to the psychic centres located along our spine, from the base of the spine. Yes, right at the bottom there, at the tail, and right up to the top and just above your head. There are ten of them and they are invisible; more like a kind of spinning energy. Well, in addition to their function as regulators or transformers of psychic energy, they also maintain the mind-body harmony or balance." I explained.

"In our next session we're going to do a procedure called 'balancing the chakras'. It's about fine tuning your mind-body engine. The severely distressing life experiences you've been through have seriously disrupted that delicate, subtle balance that is necessary for optimal functioning in the physical, mental and spiritual domains. What we'll do today are some preparatory steps that will set the stage so to speak, for you to achieve the desired level of that mind-body balance or homeostasis[21]. I will also provide you with a CD recording of the procedural steps that you are to do at home. Agreed?"

"Whatever you say, Doc. I am putting my complete trust in you. Um, Doc, how old are you? Please forgive me for asking, I'm just a little bit curious."

"That's all right, my dear child. I am old enough to be your father. As a matter of fact, my first daughter is a few years older than you are. Surprised, eh?" This rather personalized exchange came as no surprise to me, for I had, through many years of clinical practice, come across several instances of the transference[22] of feelings and emotions that often emerge between client and the therapist. At times, however, these are not so mild and easy flowing but can be punctuated by stormy, aggressive, and some-times even physical outbursts by an agitated or unstable client.

"Okay, what I would like you to do now is to keep your eyes focused on the centre of the computer screen, always on the centre point, regardless of all the moving and changing geometric patterns and colours that appear. You are seeing the whole picture and the moving patterns, but try not to be distracted from the centre point, right? Good. The softly playing music that you are hearing in the earphones is being constantly transformed into the moving figures, constantly changing yet never repeating themselves. They are always new, always different. Just keep your eyes on that centre point. Very good."

Lisa was steadily approaching a state of moderate relaxation with focused, meditative concentration, which was achieved through visual stimulation by a series of abstract geometric images moving in unison and perfect harmony with the soothing mental imagery music. This was a fairly recent application I had incorporated into the wide range of psychotherapeutic techniques we are able to choose from, as the need arises. It is generated through an innovative computer software called random alchemy, and serves as a dynamic probe of the unconscious, bringing to the fore many repressed and disturbing memories but through a medium that makes them much more tolerable and easier to manage by the client.

Lisa was instructed to voice the thoughts, ideas or words that gradually came to her mind while viewing the images. Later on, an interpretive analysis is drawn from them. After we ended the procedure, Lisa could not recall any of the thoughts that had come to her mind while viewing the moving images. Neither the words nor the memories she had just spoken out. They were all being dredged up from the unconscious, forcing her to experience considerable emotional turmoil. But by the end of the procedure, the memories had already reverted, not to the blackest caves of the unconscious mind, but a bit nearer to conscious awareness, to that area we call the preconscious mind, from whence presumably they would be available for her to recall to consciousness.

"Okay, Lisa. You won't remember all the thoughts or ideas or memories that came to you while viewing the images, at least not for now, eh? But do tell me how you felt while going through the procedure, especially during the last part."

"It is not easy to explain, Doc. At first I felt like the whole thing was pulling me into the computer screen, those moving colours and lines and circles, they're kind of weird, and I felt like they grabbed my mind, my thoughts taking me from one thing to the other. But as soon as I sort of got accustomed to looking at them, they became interesting. They're cool. It's just that you can't control them at all. It's like they are about to race and drag your mind away. They kinda want to look like a lot of rapidly opening and closing vaginas, and at times like two penises following and chasing after them. I don't know, they kept changing all the time, and so fast. Then they want to look like shooting stars falling from the sky. Real weird, though," Lisa said.

"Oh, in the last part I was feeling droopy, like the whole thing wanted to put me to sleep. My eyes were actually shutting down on me but I just had to keep my eyes open, keep looking at them. Doc, did you see me nodding?" By this time her earphones were off, but the moving kaleidoscope of random geometric shapes was still dancing away on the monitor to the tempo of the inaudible music. Lisa could not avoid looking at them.

"Can you recall a special time, a cherished moment in your life when you felt so good, so happy and really wonderful about yourself? Yes? Now, I want you to go right back into that moment and not only remember the event itself, but try to visualize yourself into it now. Try to feel the feeling, the emotions of that very special time right now. Describe those moments, just relive them and tell me in your own words."

"Hey, Doc! I find it strange that you are asking me about my greatest moment, those exciting and fabulous times in my life because strange enough, now I realize that that is exactly one of the first thing that came into my mind while I was viewing those dancing images a while ago. It was after that incident, you know… the rape, and when I broke off with Carl and went to the States for a while. Well, as you know I met a lot of nice, interesting men up there. I was looking real good then, with my nice shape and all, not with these narrow hips I have now because I've lost some weight. Oh yes, guys would just come on to me and offer to buy me a car, or give me money and anything I wanted. I mean real big men, and they would tell me that even if I am married or have a boyfriend it was no problem. All they wanted was a piece of the action every now and then. Can you imagine that, Doc?" Lisa asked. "Well, there was this attorney I met in Miami, an older gentleman. He was around sixty or so, and we became friends for a while until I foolishly came back to Jamaica and got myself stuck in a marriage to Carl Anthony. But this fellow, the attorney, he really knew how to make me feel good about myself, in every way, Doc. Each and every time. He would give me whatever I asked for. He always said that I am a goddess and how he wants to kneel at my feet to worship and adore me, and serve and obey me as my personal slave. Gosh! He used to tell me real crazy stuff like that all the time, and it would really make me feel so good like a goddess for sure."

She continued: "But this guy was kinky and wacky. After a while he got into this habit of wanting to suck my toes, even in public, like in the swimming pool in the hotel. Then he wanted me to have sex with a woman in front of him, or with him and this male friend of his. Oh, I knew he was a real sickie, but he was really nice, and when I am with him I felt like I was on top of the world, like a queen. I always remember those times, but I lost contact with him long ago, so now it is just memories."

As she was saying these words, her eyes took on a pensive, far away look, like projecting herself back in time to relive and savour the intensely satisfying sensation of supreme confidence and full awareness of her seductive powers of enchantment.

"Very good, Lisa, very good. The important thing here are the inner feelings, the emotions you experienced then. At that time, the silent, subjective talk or chatter that constantly goes on inside your mind is not only reflecting your mood and the circumstances around you then, but they are also setting the tone and the vibrations of your nervous system and of your entire body", I said. "So, what we need to do is to recapture and then constantly practise, the *feeling* and the *words* we were telling ourselves then, and make them a permanent part of our being, that is, internalize them so deeply that you can routinely bring up the feelings, the words, and the whole ambience of those long past moments and again become infused with that powerful good feeling."

This is the concept of neuro linguistic programming, NLP, which has been applied mainly in the areas of motivational psychology, self esteem enhancement, assertiveness training and even in sports psychology. It is now being increasingly used within the clinical setting with consistently good results. In some ways, there are similarities between NLP and basic conditioning, the main difference being that with the neuro linguistic programming techniques, the programming or conditioning takes place and operates physiologically at the cellular, neuronal level, producing measurable changes for optimal functioning, but also at the unconscious level where it would have significant positive effect on patterns of behaviour and thinking.

I wondered if Lisa would have the self-discipline and diligence to practise, incorporate and adopt this rather simple technique of reorienting her attitudinal disposition towards herself and her world. The success and duration of our intervention would depend, to some extent, on her level of dedication to this technique and to the other procedures as well.

○

"Good afternoon, sir. I am so sorry to be late, but I didn't drive myself this time and Carl had many stops to make before getting here. He said he'd come to see you next week. At least that's what he says. Well, thank God I am here in one piece, safe and sound. And how are you, Doc? You always look so cool and calm, like you are under no pressure at all, and no problems. But then, who do you go to when you have your personal problems, Doc? To one of your colleagues or so?" she asked amidst her bubbly laughter and apparent delight and relief at another opportunity to freely unburden herself of the psychic and emotional baggage she'd been carrying around for so long.

"Oh no, Lisa, I wouldn't do that at all. Never did, although my wife used to take perverse joy in lovingly admonishing me with gems like '*You are a sick man. You are mentally sick. You don't even realize that you need professional help. I am going to ask your good friend, Doctor so and so to provide you with some urgent help…*' Of course my mental illness in her book, is not agreeing to some opinion or other of hers."

"That's funny, for sure. Um, Doc, there is a question, a technical question I have for you. But lest I forget, I brought something to show you. Here, you can look at these." She handed me an envelope containing about a dozen or so family photographs, mostly wedding photos, which I closely examined with undisguised admiration.

"Thanks, I really do appreciate you sharing these precious mementoes with me. They are all lovely photos. You both make a beautiful couple." Lisa looked at me slightly surprised by my words, but quickly recovered and said, "Well yes, that's true. But don't let him fool you, Doc; everybody likes him and he always tries to show that he is Mr. Nice Guy. You know, the charmer. But as they say out there, *to know me, and to come live with me, are two different things, eh?* You will see for your-self, Doc, when you meet him next week."

For a few silent moments, she looked pensive and distant, like reviewing thoughts, memories, and past impressions in her mind, most likely related to her husband.

"Lisa, you did say that you had a question you wanted to ask me. Please go ahead, ask and let us see if I can give you an answer."

"Yes, Doc. I just want to hear what you have to say to this. Between a man and a woman, when they are making love, which of the two feels the greater, more intense pleasure, the man or the woman?"

"Wow, that's a tough one, lady. I can only give you a kind of rhetorical answer, okay? Now, when your ear itches deep inside and you insert and wiggle your little finger in it, where do you feel the sweet relief of pleasure, on the finger, or in the ear?" Though I had responded by posing a question, there was only one possible honest reply to it, one that would, by analogy, also answer her original question.

"Oh! You mean it's *the woman* who experiences the greater pleasure? Really now. I like that about the ear and the finger, ha, ha, ha. But, why? I mean, what's the reason or the cause. Why is it so and not the other way around?" Lisa queried.

"It's just that we are made up differently in many ways, yet we are still both very similar in our humanity. Like for example, in a woman her sexuality is disseminated throughout her whole body. All of her body is one total erogenous zone with an organic need to be sexually stimulated. If this need is thwarted or remains unfulfilled, she becomes frustrated, resentful and embittered," I explained.

"But in the man, his erogenous zones are concentrated almost exclusively in three areas: the oral, the genital, and the anal. These correspond to the sites of psychosexual stages of development in babyhood and infancy, according to Sigmund Freud..., and..."

"Freud? I read something about him and his crazy ideas..., he was a madman. Isn't he the one who said that all women suffer from some kind of penis envy towards men? And that daughters are sexually attracted to their fathers and are in competition with their mothers, eh?" she interjected vigorously.

"Well, yes. That's the *Electra* complex in little girls; in little boys, it's the *Oedipus* complex, that brief stage during which he's sexually attracted to his mother and is in rivalry with his father. I do agree that some of his concepts were, and still are, very controversial. But many of his theories are quite valid and accepted," I offered, perhaps a bit lamely given her assertive and pugnacious stance while she looked at me with a wide, triumphant smile.

"There are other significant differences too between a man and a woman, biological and otherwise. In the interplay between the sexes, a man's weakness is *in his eyes*, his vision. He's primarily attracted to what he sees, thereby his appetite for visual erotica, the nude female body, and pornography. A woman's weakness, though is *in her ears*, in hearing the whispered words of adulation and flattery, of promises, of undying love. It's what she falls for over and over again."

I then explained the differences in brain function, whereby women think mostly with the right half and men predominantly with the left. Let's try to get back to the schedule for the session, okay? Good. Now let me ask you this Lisa: On a scale of one to ten, what number would you assign to your level of happiness and satisfaction in your marriage? Think about it for a while and tell me."

"I don't need to think about it at all, Doc. I can tell you right away. It is zero, nought. Yes, I am serious about that, Doc. It's been about four months since Carl and I had sex. My whole life has become so boring. He seems to have lost interest, too, and to make things worse, when it comes to sex he has always been found wanting, if you know what I mean. Foreplay? I wonder if he even knows the meaning of the word, much less," Lisa remarked.

"I looove oral sex, real bad. But Carl, he is so inept and clumsy, he just doesn't have a flair for it. I've tried with him for so long, patiently teaching and coaching him. I have to tell him, *'No Carl, come up a little higher..., no, no, not so high, you ..., go back, stay there.* I tell you, it's frustrating, really pathetic. It's like having brain surgery performed by a barber! You know what I mean..., ha, ha, or like having your expensive luxury sports car being worked on by an apprentice roadside mechanic."

There was strong but subdued passion in her expressive facial, eyes, and body movement, with everything coming across very convincingly, even amidst the sarcastic, humorous analogies she so cleverly applied.

"And you know what, Doc? I am a good woman, maybe too damn good for Carl. He doesn't deserve a woman like me. He just doesn't appreciate me, doesn't know what he has. Most other women would be giving him bun[23] and more bun. Left, right, and centre and around the clock. But I am not like that. I'm not the type to do that. I've been faithful to him, well, even before we got married," Lisa said assertively.

"It is very good that you lived by the moral principles and the vows of faithfulness you had taken. Yet, you describe a situation of frustration and much unhappiness in your marriage. In our next session, when I meet with you both, we will revisit, carefully explore and try to deal further with that aspect of your life issues. At this time we will proceed with the first steps in balancing the chakras. You will continue with the CD instructional guide at home, okay? Now, please start breathing rhythmically in, and slowly out, again in…, slowly out…, good…, your eyes are closing by themselves…, yes, it is dark, very dark…, and in the darkness you see a bright, very big number. The number is 100, and it is all in one color, your favorite color. Now, let us slowly…, very slowly, start counting *back*, counting *backwards*, and the colors change with each number, and each number has a different color…, 99.., 98.., 97…, 96…, 95…"

With this concept and application of balancing the chakras, the objective was for Lisa to correct or repair, the acquired warp or defect in her aura[24] that originated with the rape experience she underwent. This psychic scarring had formed in her a disposition or unconscious attitude of being victim prone, with a propensity towards instinctively and perhaps too readily, playing the victim role when and if she finds herself in even slightly similar circumstances to the rape ordeal.

Recent research has shown that, statistically, a woman who has been raped once, is twice as likely to be raped again compared to a woman who has never been raped. Oftentimes, it is because the potential repeat victim exudes a certain effulgence of fear in their aura that can be felt, albeit unconsciously, by a potential aggressor, who is sensitive enough to discern or intuit the subtle promptings of apprehensive expectation. Those signs may be psychic, or sensory, like a smell, or a look of incipient trepidation in the eyes, a fearful willingness to submit, or may be betrayed by sudden, confused, or clumsy body movements.

She had slowly arrived at number 81, pink, and then barely plodded on to number 76, red, where she fell silent while still maintaining a steady breathing pattern. A few more steps in the procedure, involving mainly a reversing of the first stage, plus a brief application of the Quantum Touch healing hands technique, concluded the session. I stressed the importance of diligently doing the subsequent steps at home, as outlined in the instructional CD, to which she promised faithful compliance.

Two days later, I got a phone call from Lisa's mother, Mrs. Silvia Stetzmann, who was evidently very concerned about her daughter's condition, her mental state as she put it.

"I really don't know what else to do to help Lisa, this is something that has been going on for so long, Doc, from she was a teenager. She has been constant bad news for me and for the rest of the family. She didn't grow up with me, but mostly with my mother from since she was seven. She was very close to her grandmother. Ever since the death of Grandma, Lisa has been acting erratically, taking all kinds of unnecessary risks in her life. And, Doc, she has such a temper. I am afraid that one of these days she will hurt someone, or Carl, or herself."

"Has she ever displayed violent behaviour, or maybe physically hurt someone, or attempted to harm, or kill herself? I asked.

"Doc, I knew she wouldn't disclose certain things to you, or reveal the truth about herself. About a year ago, she almost killed a cousin of mine, a far relative of hers, jumped on the young lad screaming and biting, almost gouged one of his eyes out over a minor dispute about a TV channel or so. Twice she tried to commit suicide. After my mom died she tried to drown herself, and then just two years ago it was an overdose of sleeping pills after an argument with Carl. She's always hurling threats and insults, and has gotten into this habit of cursing and using the most disgraceful language, like she's out of her mind. I don't know why she insists on hiding these things from her therapist if she really wants help…, for god's sake…"

"Now, Mrs. Stetzmann, do you know what caused the argument they had? The one that brought about the sleeping pills attempt?" I asked.

"Oh, that was some foolishness about a business client of his, a lady, who Lisa claims he was having an affair with. Carl is an accountant and does most of his work from home, so that was just an excuse of hers to get to that poor man. She's always saying that I am taking sides with Carl, but he is a good man, a decent fellow and he has been trying with her all these years.

She's my first child, and I love her dearly, but her behavior is terrible, she's driving us all crazy," the mother said.

She continued: "What I really wanted to talk to you about, Doc, is the fact that I think Lisa may need some kind of stronger or more radical treatment. Over the years, nothing they've tried seems to work with her, to just cool her down, slow her down a bit. There's this lady I met in church recently and she was telling me about her son and how his condition was very much like Lisa's, and nothing helped him much until they used the shock treatment on him at the hospital, and he has improved so much since. Do you think that this shock thing could help my daughter?"

Hers was a troubled voice that came across as being awash in unmitigated anguish, pregnant with doom in her unbridled concern for her daughter's welfare and future prospects of living a normal, sedate life. And although I had a client coming in shortly, I decided to stay a little longer on the phone with the good lady, explaining the pros and cons of this particular treatment option.

"Ms. Silvia, you are referring to ECT or electro-convulsive therapy. This is a form of therapy in which the physician places electrodes on the patient's temples, and an electric current goes through the brain for about one second. The objective is to bring about a brief seizure in the entire body lasting around twenty seconds, and this is done three times a week for several weeks. It works in cases of severe depression, especially those that do not respond to other forms of therapy," I explained.

"Several factors must be considered before the clinician decides to apply ECT, because there are important risks involved, like loss of certain forms of memory, and even though the procedure itself is not a painful one, many patients are terrified at the prospect of undergoing such therapy. But then, that is a decision that a psychiatrist at the hospital would have to make, according to his clinical judgment in the case.

I think we should allow some more time for the therapies we're currently using with Lisa to work out their healing potential, and see how she responds to the procedures, okay? In the meantime, I would encourage you to be patient and supportive of your daughter, regardless of how obnoxious and detestable her behavior may be. To know that she is loved, wanted and accepted by those who are close to her, can play an important role in her recovery," I added.

After exchanging pleasantries, we ended the conversation with a mutual promise not to give up on her daughter, but to persist in our determination to help her in whichever way possible.

✿

"Mr. Carl Bryant is here to see you, sir. No, sir, it is just Mr. Bryant; Miss Lisa called earlier and changed her appointment for Friday at three in the afternoon. Should I send him in now?"

"Oh yes, certainly, Mrs. Ferguson." I replied, while inevitably wondering about the cause for the sudden change in the previous arrangement I had, which was to conduct a joint session with the couple.

"Pleased to meet you, Doc. I must apologize because my wife decided at the last minute that she doesn't want to come along with me. She didn't give any reason. She called and made another appointment, so I thought it was best if I still kept the one we had for today if it's okay with you, sir," he explained, while taking a seat I had indicated to him.

"Oh sure, that's quite all right, Mr. Bryant. Nice to meet you, too. It is good that you decided to come nevertheless. And how is Lady Lisa Nicola doing, eh?" I asked.

"Well, I don't know what to say. For the past week or so, I would say that there is some improvement, but that happens all the time, and it doesn't last more than a week or two. I am a layman to all this but, anyone can see for themselves that something is radically wrong with Lisa, and to be honest, I am at my wits' end. I don't know what else to do," Carl said. "I am sure she told you about the incident with the two guys. Well, she tells everybody about it, even complete strangers, people she's just met. It is since that time that her behaviour has become so rotten and unpredictable, violent too. She has no friends, at all, because she doesn't get along with anybody, no one at all. She has caused me to lose several good jobs, friends and business associates. Any woman I have to interact with, like in business, she accuses me of being intimate with them. And any male friend or associate I have, she says that he is a battyman[25]. It is disgraceful, Doc, because she would lash out at me with insults and a string of bad words in front of anybody, screaming at the top of her voice."

Carl patiently outlined the features of the very challenging situation he was dealing with on an almost daily basis, while I simultaneously did a keen clinical observation and analysis of this outwardly calm, personable and very likeable fellow. And although

I recalled Lisa's warning about not allowing him to fool or charm me, I could not help but conclude that Carl Anthony was a rather reasonable and balanced individual, who was still very much in love with his beautiful but highly unstable wife.

"Just yesterday when I asked about her frequent smoking of ganja (marijuana) in the living room, she told me that it is part of the therapy, to help her to calm down. Of course, I know she's making that up, trying to excuse or cover up in some sort of a way," Carl noted.

"Well, Mr. Bryant, I take it that this whole situation has had a devastating impact on the marriage, and on you both individually. Has there been any, even minor, improvement in the quality of intimacy and communication?"

"I no longer even approach her about that, Doc, I don't know if she told you, but we've been sleeping separately now for quite a while. I sleep alone in the bedroom, not of my choosing of course, and she sleeps on the sofa in the living room clutching a pair of scissors to her chest. Yes, she is violent. She hasn't really attacked anyone yet, but one day last week she just started ranting and raving against my mother, who was next door and could not even hear her, when suddenly she took a machete and chopped the window panes, breaking several of them." While Carl Anthony was recalling his wife's furious outbursts, I noticed in his eyes that tell-tale look of trepidation and anxiety, almost like the look of disquieting fear that comes forth when one is faced with an unpredictable dark menace.

"Now, Mr. Bryant, I appreciate your deep concern with your wife's situation and the many problems associated with it, and we are trying to help her as much as possible. But what about you?

How are you managing? Are you coping all right, and do you feel strong enough to go on for the long run in bearing with her and her slow return to normality?"

I had posed these questions to Carl Anthony while carrying out an assessment of a few basic physiological indicators: arterial blood pressure, heart rate, iris analysis for toxicity, and other routine procedures to assess for perceptual and cognitive competence, all of which reflected good to excellent overall physical and mental health.

"I think I am doing quite well, maybe because after all this time I kind of understand Lisa much more than before, and I just don't allow her to stress me out to any great extent. I have learnt to control myself and I try to ignore a lot of her provocation, and just let certain things pass. Well, I can tell you that right now you are the only friend she has, like someone to talk to, because she can be so difficult most of the times. I don't want to be a pessimist, but I wouldn't be surprised if out of the blue she suddenly turns against you and shows you her vicious side. She does it all the time, over and over, no matter how nice you are to her."

As Carl was saying this I perceived an unequivocal certainty in his words, one that likely came out of his intimate and profound knowledge of the unique personality and character of his wife. I did not suspect then that his words would come to pass.

The following Friday, I had the scheduled therapy session with Lisa. It was an abbreviated one, due to an unforeseen emergency which came up that I had to go away to deal with. "And how was the past week for you, Mrs. Bryant? I trust that you managed to follow up with the instructions at home? Yes? Well, tell me about it."

"Can't really complain, Doc. For once in a long while, I had a fairly good week; Carl and I even went out. We went on a tour of the countryside in Saint Elizabeth on the South Coast. We even stopped by that famous place there, Lovers Leap, which is very interesting though a bit scary. The high cliff made me dizzy. Yes, Doc, I put on the CD and did the exercise, which of course put me to sleep again. I fell asleep with the recording going. It was Carl who came in and turned it off for me. But guess what? Well, I think I should tell you, Doc because I am not hiding anything from you; you are my therapist, so…, okay. I noticed that after I woke up I was feeling *sooo* horny, raunchy, you know what I mean, like I would just go somewhere and get on real bad with somebody, no one in particular; just get to hold him down and murder him with it. You know what I mean? To let him feel like he's having a heart attack in bed. Is this a normal reaction, Doc? You must be thinking that I am so terrible and out-of-order, right, Doc? Tell me, tell me the truth." While speaking, Lisa was constantly gesticulating and displaying a jovial, exciting mood, as if riding the high crest of a wave of libidinal energy.

"Ehm, I try my best to be non-judgmental, as you well know, my dear lady; I don't criticize, belittle, or denigrate any-one. I try instead to understand them and the reason they act and behave in certain ways. So don't worry about that, okay? The after effects you noticed are quiet normal, well, I mean, expected ones. First of all, the balancing of the chakras would quiet that part of your mind that was hyper excited, and that quieting, calming effect would be felt within your mind, body, spirit; you would be so relaxed that you would easily fall asleep," I explained. "Those heightened sexual desires or lustful cravings you felt after doing the exercise were the delayed effects of the moving images you had gazed at on the computer monitor a few days before. When those geometric images combined so that they moved together in unison, they imprinted themselves in your mind in a way that would elevate or increase your libido or life force, your psychic energy, making you feel more vibrant, more alive so to speak. Often, this higher level of psychic energy would bring about a kind of pervasive sensuality with strong desire to seduce, and so on. The overall effects are beneficial, but when it comes to the increased sex drive, you would have to apply good judgment and self control."

I was interrupted by a soft coded knock on the door. The intercom and phones were off, and the ubiquitous sign reading 'THERAPY SESSION IN PROGRESS, DON'T INTERRUPT', was on the outer door knob. The receptionist's rap on the door could only mean that the matter was important, urgent, or worse, an emergency. I decided that the tone of the knock was soft enough to mean just merely important.

"Ehm, Lisa, I think we may have to end the session for today, but let me leave you with this: the real purpose and aim of all that we have been doing to assist you, the whole therapeutic process, is essentially for you to control your mind. If you control your mind, you can control your world and those around you. In all you do, Lisa, strive for that, control your mind and everything else will follow. Okay? I am so sorry that we have to abridge the session today, but next week we'll pick up from here."

"Well, that's okay. This was a wonderful session. Thanks ever so much for taking time out to listen to me with all my bag of problems, and thanks for your help. See you next week, Doc. Take care, bye."

After she left, and having attended to the important matter outside, I returned to the office and sat quietly to make notes and review the just concluded session. That's when it dawned on me that throughout the session, Lisa had made no mention of Carl Anthony's meeting with me last week, neither did she say anything about the telephone conversation I had with her mother a few days ago. Is it that she wasn't aware that both of them had spoken to me? Had they both opted not to tell Lisa anything about their talk with me? Good reasons they might have had for keeping it from her.

✿

It was almost eleven in the night when my mobile phone started ringing for the second time. I was just coming out of the bathroom. I knew that I had missed a call when it rang about five minutes before, so most likely it was the same caller.

"Hello, good night. Who is it, please?"

"I am so disappointed in you, Doc. I wasn't expecting this from you at all. How could you?

"Hello, is this you, Mrs. Bryant? What happened, what's the matter?

"Please, please, Doc! Don't pretend! You have betrayed me in the worst way. I just got off the phone with my mother, and she told me how you are recommending the electro shock treatment for me. I thought you were on my side. I really trusted you, and see what happens? You go and join up with the old witch and that creepy pimp to have me electrocuted. I am going to have all three of you locked up." Lisa's voice level increased considerably. She wasn't yet shouting into the phone, but she was quickly getting more agitated.

"No, no, just a minute please. Lisa, I did not at any time make any such a recommendation. Your mom called me, and just enquired about it. All I did was to give her a little general information regarding ECT the electro convulsive therapy. She said she had heard someone in church talking about it, and it just came up during our telephone chat. But please, calm down, take control of your mind, Lisa," I pleaded.

"Hey, let me tell you this, Doc. I am in full control of my mind. Do you hear me? Full control! You slime ball! Imagine, after I put my trust in you, and you pretended all along that you have my best interests at heart, and 'bout you are helping me, and this and that, you are nothing but a damn traitor! I don't want to see you, and I don't want to hear from you! You ganging up with them against me? They must have bought you out! I am gonna make you smell the shit! I am gonna step on your fucking balls!" she yelled.

Lisa was furious and out of control, so I continued to listen and wait for her anger to subside. The other consideration was should I cut the call, she may go on to vent her fury on someone or something or even herself there at home. So I just kept the phone a little distance from my aching ear. I could still hear her though. And she went on to pepper me with a collection of colourful Jamaican expletives, coupled with an invitation to kiss the nethermost parts of her anatomy.

"Lisa, Lisa, please, please listen to me. I am still willing to help you. Please follow the instructions and the techniques, regardless. And please, take good care of yourself; your mom and your husband they both love you," I said.

"What did you say?! Love me? love me?! Yes, they love me dead, that's how they love me."

By this she had slightly, just barely calmed down a bit, but not enough to keep her from throwing her last evil curse at me: *"As for you, Mr. Traitor, I hope your next client turns out to be a serial killer!"*

With that, she slammed her phone shut.

❂

A few weeks passed by without any of us here at the centre hearing from the Bryants, or from Lisa's mother. It was Carl Anthony who broke the silence; he called me one morning early to tell me that his wife had almost gone berserk at home the previous evening, throwing and breaking everything in sight. She had been taken to the hospital, was medicated and stabilized, and was now with relatives in rural Saint Elizabeth resting and hopefully recuperating. They had all agreed that a change in environment would have some beneficial effect on her. He himself also yearned for a respite from the constant mental strain upon him that having Lisa around caused.

Months passed by, and gradually, other clinical challenges came to demand our attention, leading away from the remarkable case of The Girl with the Narrow Hips, which was the designated identifying code on Lisa's file. But, as always, the past does inevitably come around to haunt us, or at least to remind us that surprises can emerge from the past, even the most unforeseen ones. One morning as I was picking up a few items at one of the local pharmacies in the area, I heard giggles behind me, and suddenly two hands came around and covered my eyes. They were soft female hands, perfumed and recently manicured.

"Okay, I give up. Who is it?" The hands came off, I turned around to see a smiling Lisa standing before me, tall, lovely, and immaculately dressed.

"Hey, it's me, Doc. It's me. Oh, am I happy to see you. This is my friend Camille, I have told her so much about you. Camille, this is Doctor Brooks, my therapist; the one you hear me talking so much about. He's the one that saved my life. Doc, I saw you on TV sometime last month, on the news about that case with the woman and her sons. You are looking great, as always. Not one day older. You have to give me the secret. *Pleeease*, Doc, will you?" Lisa asked.

"Ah, but I am sure that I gave you that secret long ago. Remember? Well, well, this is really such a nice surprise. I am so pleased to see you too, Lisa. You are looking great, fantastic. And how are you doing? And how is Carl?" I asked, sharing in the contagious excitement of the moment.

"I can't complain, Doc. For the past four months I've been working with this engineering firm in Kingston, and I am getting on pretty well there. I've already got a minor promotion too, and things look promising for me there. Carl is quite all right, too. He's not doing badly at all. He's got some big projects working on now. He is planning to give you a call soon, one of these days, but we know that you are always so busy. I'll tell him that I saw you. Would you believe that I still practise the meditation, the breathing exercises, and all the other stuff you showed me. Well, as often as I can. I am going to come to look for you soon, Doc."

"That's wonderful. Just don't give them up completely, Lisa and do continue to practise the procedures as often as you can, okay? Give Carl Anthony my regards and my blessing, and best wishes to you both. Be strong now."

And as Lisa and Camille laughingly sauntered out the door, giving one last glance and wave, I realized that I had completely forgotten what I needed to buy. The surprising encounter had momentarily psyched me out.

The End

NOTES

1 Dirección de los Servicios de Inteligencia y Prevención, Directorate of Intelligence and Prevention Services, is the main intelligence gathering and analysis organization within Venezuela's security and police apparatus. It evolved in the 1970's from its direct predecessor of the days of the dictator Pérez Jiménez, the dreaded DIGEPOL or Dirección General de Policía, whose brutally efficient operatives and agents had earned for themselves a most feared reputation, both amongst the opponents of the regime, and also within the nation's criminal underworld.

2 Escuela de Mecánica de la Armada, Navy Mechanics School, infamous torture center on Avenida Libertador in Buenos Aires, where thousands of suspected leftists and even mere sympathizers were murdered during Argentina's so called 'dirty war' during the military dictatorship of the 1980's.

3 Based largely on the pioneering work of Milton H. Erickson, Ericksonian psychotherapy is founded on technique and is based on the assumption that there is an unconscious mind that may be accessed and mobilized to produce psychological relief. Symbols and ambiguity are used through indirect techniques of clinical hypnosis to stimulate and activate previously dormant strengths from within the patient. Its fundamental objective is to facilitate optimal levels of mind-body integration.

4 Women's wearing of erotic mini garments with long cords that are tightly laced around legs, torso and arms to enhance the erotic allure of rounded flesh bulging under the tight laces.

5 Slang term for cocaine hydrochloride, the alkaloid crystals in powdered form, which is among the most powerful of available stimulants and in great demand as a recreational drug.

6 Rorschak inkblot test is based on projective techniques that are very sensitive to unconscious dimensions of personality. Defense mechanisms, latent impulses, anxieties and neuropsychological impairment have been inferred in projective situations. It also measures complex psychological dynamics (otherwise known

as the subconscious).

7   The TAT uses ambiguous stimuli in the form of pictures as a probe of the unconscious. The client is asked to describe the thoughts and feelings of the people in the pictures, and inference is drawn from their responses.

8   Popular slang term in Jamaican creole (patois) for marijuana. Ganja refers to India's sacred Ganges river. There it has been used for millennia to achieve exalted states of altered consciousness through an afflatus of the soul and an expansion of awareness, creativity, and contemplative introspection. It is currently the most popular, extensively used recreational drug; and though not physically addictive, it may produce in susceptible individuals various forms of psychological dependence to its effects.

9   Quaint terminology from old British law still used in Jamaica to designate an unmarried woman living with a man as his wife. A derogatory equivalent is the often heard phrase, 'they are living in open concubinage', or the haughty, self-righteous utterance, 'living in sin'.

10   A smooth metallic stud, double ended with two rounded knobs, vertically traversing the forward area of the pierced tongue. Worn mostly by prostitutes, it provides additional titillation during various forms of oral sex. The knobs are threaded, thus allowing removal or reinsertion of the tongue-stud. Its origins and extensive use has been traced to ancient Babylonian, Assyrian and Israeli harlots.

11   Succubus, a nightmarish demon assuming female form and exhibiting intense nymphomania (or uterine fire, insatiable sexual appetite) having exhausting sexual intercourse with men in their sleep and draining them of their seminal fluid. The experience usually leaves the victim with a chronic ejaculatory drip often lasting several days.

12   From the Greek Psyche, mind; that which has a mental origin or basis such as conflicts or complexes. Happening subjectively, that is, entirely within the mind.

13   A chronic, degenerative, slowly progressive undulating disease of the central nervous system; not fatal, but is ineluctably numbing, crippling and paralyzing as it advances. The etiology (cause) is unknown and there is no specific therapy. So far, there is no known cure for MS.

14   Anorgasmia: a sexual difficulty involving the absence of orgasm in women. Generalized lifelong anorgasmia refers to a female who has never experienced orgasm (sexual climax) by any means.

15 'Engrams' are hypothesized physical changes that take place in the brain as it stores information; a memory trace.

16 Progressive resistance vaginal exercise for the functional restoration of the perineal muscles. Developed by Dr. Arnold H. Kegel, MD, they strengthen the pelvic floor and clear capillaries of fatty buildup, thereby making orgasm easier to arrive at. The squeeze technique prescribed consists of three consecutive pelvic-vaginal squeezes, then one longer squeeze, to be repeated say ten times or more per day, at random times.

17 In this case it was a depressed mood of sustained, pervasive feelings of despair that does not dissipate and is unresponsive to treatment. Prominent symptom is a subjective feeling of intense sadness.

18 One of the anxiety disorders showing excessive and uncontrollable worry about various events or activities representing unclear or ambiguous threats, and also showing other symptoms such as restlessness, muscle tension, and sleep disturbance.

19 Narcissistic Personality Disorder. Obsessive self love or self admiration at times manifesting as sexual pleasure derived from contemplating one's own naked body. From Narcissus; Greek mythological character who fell in love with his own image reflected in a water pond.

20 Borderline Personality Disorder. An enduring pattern of thinking and behaviour showing a pervasive instability in mood, emotions, self-image, and interpersonal relationships. Other characteristics are a marked tendency to impulsivity and poor decision making ability.

21 A state of dynamic equilibrium of the internal environment of the body in its relationship with the mind. It is maintained through an integrated process of feedback and regulation that is mediated by the psychic centres or Chakras located at specific points along the vertebral column (central nervous system).

22 A mental process by which a client transfers patterns of feelings and behaviour they had previously experienced with key figures in their lives. Often these feelings, good or bad, are shifted unto the analyst.

23 To 'burn' the man; in Jamaican patois, to 'bun him', or to give him 'bun'. Cheating; marital infidelity or extra marital sex.

24 Aura. A subtle, electromagnetic effulgence that surrounds and radiates outwards from living bodies. Ordinarily invisible, it can be detected with advanced instrumentation or may be felt as subjective sensations, of a psychic nature.

The aura's strength, color, and the distance it projects from the body are indicative of the state of mind-body balance, and the level of energy and sensitivity of the psychic centers or Chakras. It is said that dogs and other animals can sense fear or boldness through one's aura.

25   Battyman. Jamaican term for male homosexual.

LUCREZIA BORGIA

A Woman of Royalty
(1480 - 1519)

She is undoubtedly one of the most celebrated luminaries of the Roman aristocracy, a woman of mystery and sophisticated allure whose seductive enchantment has persisted even through the centuries. In her short and chaotic life she fully epitomized the multiple personality facets and obvious moral instabilities of a depraved and dissolute ruling class, corrupted by the absolute power and vast wealth at their disposal.

Lucrezia Borgia was a princess of Rome and also a princess of the Roman church, reflecting as such one of the many contradictory dualities in her person and in her life. Born into the legendary Borgia dynasty, then the most powerful princely house in Italy, Lucrezia was the daughter of Cardinal Rodrigo Borgia (who later became Pope Alexander VI) and his mistress, Vannozza de Cattanei. She had been promised in marriage to powerful noble men from as early as the age of eleven, but was first married only after her father became Pope Alexander VI when she was fourteen.

At around that time Lucrezia was living in a palace right next to the Vatican along with the Pope's new mistress, Giulia Farnese, which was a very convenient arrangement that allowed the pontiff to visit them both regularly. During this time it became known that apart from serving as her father's hostess at official and diplomatic receptions, she also carried on incestuous relationships with both her father and her brothers César and Giovanni Borgia.

Along with the decadent, orgiastic revelry and the luxurious excesses of Alexander's court, the intrigues, machinations, poisonings, and assassinations were frequent happenings in which Lucrezia was either an active participant or the hidden manipulator behind the scenes. Some historians have dubbed her, perhaps unjustifiably so, the Mother of Poisoning.

When her first marriage to the nephew of Cardinal Ascanio Sforza in 1492 was no longer politically and strategically useful, the husband was forced, under threat of life, to sign a *confession of impotence* after which the Pope issued an annulment of the marriage on the basis of non-consummation. She had also been ceremoniously 'examined' by Vatican judges who confirmed that she was *intacta*, that is, still a virgin.

Lucrezia retired to a nearby convent, communicating with her father through a young servant, Perotto, with whom she committed adultery while in the convent and became pregnant. When her brother César discovered his sister's pregnancy, in a fit of fury he attacked young Perotto with his sword, stabbing him as he knelt before the papal throne, splashing Perotto's blood on his father. The young chamberlain survived that attack, but a week later his body was pulled out of the river Tiber along with the body of Lucrezia's chambermaid who was believed to have facilitated the affair.

Three years after the child had been born in secret, he surfaced under the claim that he was the son of César Borgia and an unknown woman. Shortly after, however, a papal bull was issued in which it was acknowledged that the child was the son of the Pope himself. It is said that Lucrezia insisted on having the papal bull issued because she didn't know which of her two lovers, her father or her brother, had actually fathered the child. Later on Lucrezia would refer to him as her 'half brother'. It has not been firmly established whether the child was indeed the son of Alexander, produced through incest, or the fruit of Lucrezia's 'moment of indiscretion' with the unfortunate Perotto.

Both her father and her brother César were keen on arranging another profitable marriage for Lucrezia, this time, if possible, to royalty. A few months later, she was indeed married to Alfonso, Prince of Aragón. They were both seventeen years old. But the changing vagaries of political and military alliances soon caused Alfonso to find himself and his family suddenly aligned with enemies of the papal state.

Shortly thereafter, Lucrezia's brother, César, with her full knowledge and consent, arranged the murder of this second husband who died, strangled to death on the very matrimonial bed. She was just twenty-one at the time and had already been through two husbands. She had always been under the all embracing influence of her brother César, a daring, ruthless and able politician and soldier, who was anointed a Cardinal at the age of seventeen, and who was also widely believed to have assassinated his older brother Giovanni.

It was sometime after these events, that her father journeyed to Naples in order to survey recent acquisitions for the papal state, temporarily leaving the administration of the Vatican and indeed of the church itself in the hands of Lucrezia, who would in effect at the age of twenty one, be acting as the head of the entire Christendom.

Her third husband was Afonso d'Este, the Prince of Ferrara who had, understandably with great reluctance, agreed to the marriage. They had four children, but perennially restless Lucrezia, while married to the Prince also carried on a tempestuous affair with the famous poet Pietro Bembo, though her apologists claim that this was an entirely platonic relationship. Many others also found her to be an "unusual beauty with long golden hair, perfect, brilliantly white teeth, gray eyes, her bosom smooth and admirably proportioned, all in all being of graceful form," as described by Niccolo Cagnolo. Lucrezia Borgia died on the 24th of June, 1519, at the age of thirty eight from puerperal fever after giving birth to her fifth child, who had also died shortly after being born.

The Borgia family is remembered today as one of incest, adultery, sin, murder and extravagance, and Lucrezia herself as a murderess and a jezebel. Yet, in her short and intense life, the sensual appetites and her rare blend of sacred and profane love cohabited in an intimate embrace with raw animalistic passions, symbolizing the 'angel of chaos' that resides in the unfathomable depths of our own tormented souls.

The illustration of Lucrezia Borgia provided is from a painting attributed to Bartolomeo Veneziano, on display at the Gallería Borghese in Rome.

❁

About the Author

Dr. Miguel F. Brooks is a clinical and research psychologist, lecturer and public speaker, with special interest in personality disorders and cultural identity disorders. A member of several academic and philosophic societies, Brooks is a graduate of the Instituto Istmeño in Panamá and Universidad de Carabobo in Venezuela. He holds a B.Sc. degree in General Sciences and a Licentiate in Psychological Sciences (Ph.D.). He has completed postgraduate work in parapsychology, hypnotism and mental development, and is currently in private practice. Dr. Brooks is the author of several books and was awarded the Centenary Gold Medal of the Battle of Adwa by the Ethiopian Crown Council for his work in the field of Ethiopian Culture and History.

Other books by Miguel Brooks:

- Seeking: The Alchemical Cure for Cancer

- NEGUS: Majestic Tradition of Ethiopia

- Kebra Nagast: The Glory of Kings

www.ingramcontent.com/pod-product-compliance
Lightning Source LLC
Chambersburg PA
CBHW031155270326
41931CB00006B/287